Learning Theories in
Educational Practice

Learning Theories in Educational Practice:

An Integration of Psychological Theory and Educational Philosophy

OWEN E. PITTENGER
Professor of Psychology
State University College
Oswego, New York

C. THOMAS GOODING
Professor of Psychology
State University College
Oswego, New York

John Wiley & Sons, Inc., New York · London · Sydney · Toronto

6486

To those who may never be aware of the magnitude of their impact on our personal and professional behavior.

Contents

Learning Theories in
Educational Practice

SET **X**

Prologue to a Professional Dialogue

A. OUR PROBLEM: THE DIDACTIC DILEMMA

Our purpose in writing this book is to share with our readers the issues that have confronted us as psychologists involved in the professional education of teachers. The primary thrust of this book deals with bringing educational philosophy, psychological theory, and classroom practice into closer harmony.

Authors with humanistic, phenomenological biases are faced with a basic dilemma in committing to paper that which should remain a dynamic interplay between reader and writer. We recognize that the integration of philosophy and theory into a reasonable professional practice, when it is done, is a highly individualized process that should not be dictated or imposed. We also recognize our own need to communicate certain ideas that students have reported as being valuable to them in developing a personalized strategy of teaching. We hope to support and maintain your right and responsibility to think for yourself

1

by fairly presenting a variety of philosophies and theories that are relevant to the process of determining why and how one teaches. Our plan is to protect you from the excesses of our own good intentions by stating our biases at the onset and by inviting you to disagree with us when you have reason to believe that we have overstated or oversimplified the concepts presented. Within these limitations we would like to call to your attention some contemporary practices that contribute to fragmented approaches to education.

B. FASHIONING A TEACHER

Although it has often been said in educational circles that we learn by example and precept, this principle has been distorted to the point that it frequently results in warped practice. Prime examples of a good thing being overdone is evidenced in the following statements about the best way to learn to teach. (1) Do as you are told, (2) do as you have seen, or (3) do as you have done. It is not these response modes that are inadequate. In fact, probably much of our socialized behavior has its origins in these three processes. The problem lies in the fact that these methods do not serve as a foundation for effective formal instruction and learning. Like the statement, "we learn by example and precept," the inadequate assumptions cited are truisms that add nothing toward building a sound philosophical base or a systematic approach to learning as a foundation for coherent educational practice.

If teachers operate on the basis of learning to teach by doing what they are told to do by college professors, textbooks, or field supervisors, what happens in a unique situation? Is the teacher the proverbial fish out of water? In accepting the idea that a teacher can be "trained" by doing what he is told to do, what experiential foundations for engaging in the innovative teaching behavior are assumed? In like fashion, if one bases teaching on experience as a student or on what he has done as a camp leader or Sunday School teacher, he is usually forcing an irrelevant frame of reference on himself and his students.

In order to be an effective teacher one must be willing to examine his basic beliefs about the nature of man, society, and education. Teachers must examine the compatability of their assumptions about the purposes of education with the available information about how learning takes place in order to synthesize a workable approach to teaching. Without these basic progenitors of effective methodology the professional worker will be doomed to founder in a mass of ephemeral techniques and methods that may or may not fit his own personality, the needs and expectations of his students, or the demands of the situation.

C. FINDING A PHILOSOPHY

Every mentor has a philosophy of education. He may not call it by such a pretentious label, but he has some purpose in teaching as he does. A philosophy of education is a statement of the values, purposes, and reasons for the entire educational enterprise. Whether one has taken the time to think about why children should go to school or why teachers should be paid as much as truck drivers, one will have some reasons for his position. It is true that many teachers think about basic educational problems so little or in such fuzzy ways that some psychologists would prefer to describe them as having an unconscious philosophy. The fact remains that each professional has a complex set of purposes for teaching as he does, even when the purposes are not verbalized or made explicit.

Everybody behaves consistently with the pattern of values and beliefs he holds. This is as true of teachers as it is of anyone else. If the educator's beliefs and values are inconsistent, chances are his behavior is going to be interpreted as confused and confusing. On the other hand, if his behavior is based on a coherent rationale, he is more likely to be perceived as a reasonable person whom students can respect, understand, and work with in the educational setting. Some educators use the artful dodge of relying on new ideas and common-sense interpretations of conventional techniques as a substitute for understanding the basis of their educational practices. People who try to improve education

3

without examining philosophical assumptions usually produce freaky fads, superficial systems, and culturally irrelevant fashions in education. A number of suspect positions and practices are presented for your critical evaluation in Set Six, "Procrustean Predilections or Popular Hang-Ups in Education."

D. FITTING A THEORY

Educational and psychological theoreticians have been criticized for not providing theories of learning and behavior that can be applied readily to human learning or normal classroom instruction. We agree that theories are imperfect and far from simple to apply. However, let us examine what has been substituted for a systematic approach to behavior. In the absence of an organized set of constructs describing learning the classroom has become inundated in a morass of irrelevant teaching techniques. At best, scientifically unfounded techniques are fragmentary and at worst they inhibit rather than facilitate learning. Their inconsistency and lack of concordance with a definitive philosophy results in a mixed bag of shortcuts and tricks. Few methods are clearly "bad" or fail to produce some sort of results. The critical question is: Do such methods systematically produce results consistent with a well-defined philosophy? Theories of learning and behavior provide a clear-cut concise statement of what we know about how people learn. For the educator, this statement then becomes the means of deriving effective day to day ways of teaching.

E. OUR CONTRIBUTION TO YOUR DECISION

For us the best philosophy is transactional. The best theory is phenomenological. The best teaching techniques are those that actively involve the learner in the continuing process of interactive differentiations of his perceptual field.

After you have interacted with this book you may be able

to decide the extent to which you agree with our personal commitment to this combination of philosophy, theory, and practice. In case you perceive yourself as a unique individual with the right to choose a personal perception of educational purposes and functions, we have devoted three-quarters of the book to a presentation of other philosophies, theories, and educational practices.

The extent to which you agree or disagree with our bias should be but incidental in your process of defining and committing yourself to a firmer foundation for professional behavior in whatever mode you see as most relevant to your consciously selected educational goals. Our ultimate aspiration is that you will believe in your choice and act on your commitment just as vigorously as we support and act on ours.

SET Y

Purpose, Limits, and Overview

For those of you who have not yet read Set X, this volume is addressed to the student of psychology and education who is concerned with systematic interpretations of the human learning process within the limits of the formal learning situation. It is our intention to be direct and concise, so that the inexperienced reader will have a chance to economically develop an overview of the generic bases of educational practice. In reconciling the original ideas of basic philosophies and theories, the advanced student may begin to tie together the various courses in psychology and education that he may have in his professional background and to assess the impact of these conceptualizations on his teaching behavior.

The purpose of our content and method of presentations is threefold.

1. To describe some selected philosophies of education that are in current usage in the public schools of this country and to indicate how each of them imposes certain limitations on the learning situation.
2. To describe certain theories of learning and make

7

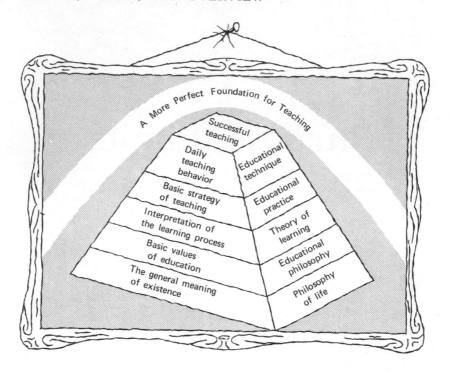

explicit the implied assumptions about the nature of man and the conditions that promote learning. This information will be derived from experimental and theoretical statements about the nature of learning.

3. To indicate the relationships of the various philosophies and theories presented. In some cases, we shall point out obvious difficulties in certain pairings, and show the relative harmony of other pairings.

The expected outcome of this essential analytical experience should be an increased sensitivity to the complexity of taking a position on the role of formal instruction and the development of a consistent systematic attitude toward learning.

The fact that the philosophies are inadequate to encompass all the values inherent in a formal program of schooling or that the theories of learning are incomplete, has not deterred us from assuming that the educator's philosophy of education should be in harmony with his theory of learning and that both should be consistent with his practice of teaching.

As we have stated in Set X, the reader may begin with whatever part of this volume he perceives is relevant. To make sure that you do not assume that the book is to be read in a particular order, we have not labeled our functional segments as conventional "chapters," which imply a fixed or recommended sequence. Each section is designed to present and to develop selected key concepts related to different aspects of understanding educational practice. Your task is to determine which section has the highest priority for you.

We have organized the book according to our needs. This does not mean that you will necessarily have the same perception of problems, issues, and organization of content.

If, after having read this book, the reader has developed better defined and more complex questions about the formal learning process, our ends will have been served.

The Authors' Position

In our view a person who is seeking to operate effectively on a professional level as an educator is actively attempting to make his philosophical assumptions explicit. He is integrating a learning theory consistent with his assumptions. He is developing methods and practices derived from the above systematic bases.

Philosophy as a series of statements of ideas concerning ontology, epistemology, and axiology can be validated through the application of logic. Any statement of reality, knowledge, and values is not enough to provide people with all the insight and information they need to develop effective educational practice. On the other hand, any attempt to derive a practice that is not fundamentally based on a coherent statement of reality, knowledge, and values cannot be systematically evaluated.

A statement of philosophy tells us where we are trying to go. In the following example, we can see what would happen if we were to take a trip without some statement of purpose:

We: "Did you have a fine trip?"
He: "Yes. I went!"
We: "Where did you go?"

11

He: "I don't know, but it was a swell trip!"
We: "Did you do what you wanted to do?"
He: "I guess so!"

It is obvious from this example that unless a person highly values a meaningless experience he must have some notion of what he intends to do. In education, philosophy provides this statement of intention.

Philosophy is primarily concerned with ends, goals, and purposes. The sciences mothered by philosophy must provide the information with which to solve the problems of the human predicament.

Knowing where you wish to go without knowing the avenues available for reaching the goal would result in random attempts to approximate a goal or a reliance on luck or magic.

The following conversation might take place if our travelers had a philosophy but not a science:

We: "Where are you going?"
He: "To Yellowstone Park."
We: "How are you going to get there?"
He: "I don't know. Here comes a bus. I think I will get on it and ride for a while and see if I get there."

We, therefore, have to evaluate goals using the methods of logic and evaluate means using the methods of science. Sound educational practice is derived from specific scientific information collected within a philosophical framework.

Since all socially significant science rests on a philosophical base, the fundamental beliefs one holds will inevitably determine which problems will be studied and which methods of science will be used.

Psychology as a behavioral science prominently associated with educational philosophy has generated a number of learning theories founded on a variety of philosophical assumptions concerning human nature. Interpretation and application of the findings of psychology has led to the postulation of numerous instructional methods dealing with the various problems of promoting human learning. Curiously, *all* methods developed to date do work—to a degree at least. Although we are personally

READY TO GO WITH THE BEST OF EVERYTHING.

most strongly identified with field theory in psychology, we do not assume that it is "best" for all educators. Our philosophical convictions are transactive in nature. Scholars, scientists, and educators whom we both respect are vigorously committed to other philosophical orientations. Given the state of psychology as a science today, the critical philosophical reexamination of man, society, and education, and the fact that any system can be made to work to some end, we cannot permit this book to become a narrow presentation of our personal commitments. Our purpose is to promote the effective integration of compatible learning theory and educational philosophy more than it is to present a closed case for any one combination. However, we shall attempt to support our belief that a gentle, indiscriminate stirring together of theory and philosophy cannot serve as an adequate basis for the development of a socially significant solution for contemporary educational problems.

Certainly, it is beyond the scope of this book to attempt to suggest specific solutions to the crucial problems facing the educators today. These problems, however, are not unrelated to this volume since the psychological theory one adheres to with its philosophical assumptions suggests characteristically relevant ways of resolving issues.

Since we do not offer specific solutions, what do we offer? Namely this: A way of attacking problems derived from consistent sets of philosophical assumptions and psychological

13

systems of human behavior. From these systems and their assumptions we shall attempt to delineate, not methods per se, but approaches to areas of learning as a model for the reader to use in synthesizing his own personal educational philosophy and learning theory.

Fads, Fictions, Fashions, and Facts

A. COMPONENTS OF EDUCATIONAL PRACTICE

The word teaching has come through poor usage to mean those things a teacher does while he is getting paid for being in a classroom. For us this definition is quite unacceptable; rather than change the conventional meaning of a common word, we propose to use another term that has not yet been so distorted. Educational practice, as we shall now use the term, will mean all of those things a teacher does to facilitate the learning process. Our explicit criteria for the effectiveness of teaching will not be how active the teacher was, but how involved and productive were the learners. Since we have dismissed all of the proper things that teachers do, all of the nice things they do, all of the sacrificial exercises they engage in that do not result in student involvement or productivity, we can also dismiss the moral basis for such behaviors as well.

Because other teachers have done it, because other teachers are doing it, because the administration said to do it, or because the children would like it, do not serve as adequate reasons for

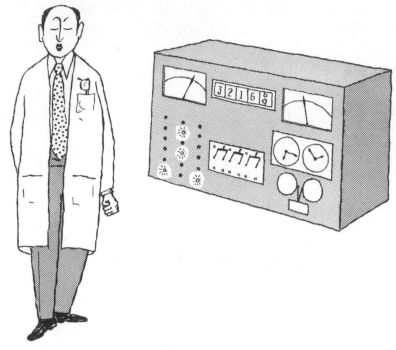

IT WORKS!

any educational practice. Unless the students are involved and productive as a result of the teacher's behavior, he can make no claim of having used an educational technique in his educational practice.

A far more subtle error, more insidious because it is at once so obvious and yet so disguised, is the justification, "it works." Many things will work, but somewhere, sometime one must ask, "Is what happens a good thing?" If we skip this important question, then we must find ourselves admiring Fagin's school for pickpockets and thieves. Except for one notable failure, it did work. He had one of the smoothest operations in town. Obviously the nature of the institution need not be questioned if the product is not too bad. Yet few parents would approve of the formal establishment of this type of institutionalized training. One must ask where children are learning to respond to educational

16

opportunities by cutthroat competitiveness, by cheating, and in too many cases, by dropping out. The reader must decide for himself whether conventional (philosophically and psychologically sloppy) teaching is "working."

Doing anything that works must also be examined with the utmost caution if we are concerned about the type of experiences our children have and the values they derive from those experiences.

ISSUES AND QUESTIONS

Every philosophy, every theory of human behavior, every experiment, every practice must rest on a set of basic assumptions. These assumptions are extremely important, since they represent a kind of subjective delineation of goals, values, and purposes for a given endeavor.

The scope of this book is limited to a consideration of selected questions that will be dealt with from the point of view of each of three prevailing frames of reference found in American education today. Certainly this effort should not be assumed to be an exhaustive treatment of philosophical issues in education. Rather, we wish to raise some significant questions about basic issues in education. This will provide the reader with an opportunity to examine the questions with regard to the array of philosophical assumptions made in arriving at different answers. We shall show that these basic assumptions either fit, partially fit, or fail to fit with particular psychological theories of behavior.

Five major questions will serve to represent the spectrum of concerns that should be vital to every professional educator.

ARE MAN AND SOCIETY FIXED INSTITUTIONS?

Any study of the human endeavor must include two dimensions—that of the import on man alone and the import on man in a group. If man is to learn, if society is to learn, this learning can only be done within the lawful limits of the nature of the

17

THE INSTITUTIONAL DILEMMA: IS IT BETTER TO CHANGE
EVERYTHING OR TO CHANGE NOTHING AT ALL?

organism. Before we can proscribe the nature of the learning
process and the nature of the teaching process, we have to know
the limits imposed on us by the learner. If society is a changing
institution with evolving values, then education will have a function quite different from its function in a stable and static society.
If man's nature is fixed by genetic factors, then teaching that
person will involve a different process than it would in the case
of a person who is only minimally restricted by genetic factors
and primarily is an open system. In any case, one's notion of
the nature of man and society limits the assumptions one can
make about learning and the teaching process.

What Should the Educative Process Do for Society?

Formal education has been institutionalized by every literate
culture in the history of man. As an institution of the society,

education has to serve society in some fashion or it will not be supported financially. There are three main interpretations of what education should do for society.

1. Education should help us preserve and rediscover the timeless values in a contemporary society.
2. Education should contribute to the improvement of our society by helping us refine our goals and techniques through the use of the best philosophical and scientific means now available.
3. Education should promote a constantly improving society in which goals and techniques are reevaluated and expanded continually.

A simple evaluation of each of these positions indicates that education has different tasks to accomplish if each of these ends are to be met. It is equally apparent that any attempt to have education serve more than one of these ends would result in a society with many verbalized responses to the purposes of education but few, if any, ethical or financial commitments.

What Should Education Do for the Individual?

At the social level, the purpose of education for the individual lends itself to the development of three answers to this question.

1. Education should prepare a man to find and fulfill his prescribed role and station in a stable society.
2. Education should prepare a man to find and fulfill a role and station for himself within the limits of his ability to contribute to an improving society.
3. Education should prepare a man to discover and fulfill his changing relationships within a growing society.

Until we know what education should do for a man we cannot begin educating him. Neither theory nor practice have within them the essence of purpose, except as derived from an underlying philosophy. Unless we select a task based on a value system, we find ourselves the slaves of and sometimes the victims of mossback traditions or ephemeral fads in the educational enterprise.

WHAT IS THE SOURCE OF AUTHORITY IN EDUCATION?

Before an educator can specify what he will or will not do, he must be aware of the nature and the scope of his authority to determine policy, make decisions, and institute action. To show how this could influence educational practice, let each reader answer the following question. What is the proper behavior for the teacher who wishes to institute a new teaching technique if he believes:

1. That his superiors have authority derived from a system of ethics that permits him only to accept their interpretations?
2. That school policies were established by men better trained than he in scientific educational research?
3. That he is a member of a team that has the responsibility for constantly appraising the value of current methods in education and participating in the search for more effective ways of teaching children?

A different procedure would be appropriate under each of these circumstances. What would make a person an innovator in one situation would make him either a troublemaker or an upstart in the others. In effect, the answer to this question specifies the limits of responsible professional participation.

HOW ARE THE NATURE AND CONTENT OF THE CURRICULUM DERIVED?

Up to this point we have suggested that the purpose of education and the teacher's role are a function of his philosophy. It is also true that what a person believes valuable enough to be taught is dictated by his convictions. The easiest way to suggest the philosophical dimensions of a curriculum problem is to ask the following question. What would a teacher do about initiating a new unit of study if:

1. The present curriculum is an orderly presentation of eternal truth?
2. The present curriculum has been logically established and carefully ordered by scientists who have studied the sociology of our society and the psychology of our children and determined that each unit as now taught is vital?
3. The curriculum is an expression of the concern of the school, the staff, and the children for the investigation of today's problems, which are in some ways different from those examined yesterday.

Although each of these positions may have been exaggerated for emphasis, it is hoped that the reader can readily see that each of the teachers cited above would have a different set of obligations in curriculum development if he were to be true to his beliefs.

SET TWO

Formulations

In this section consider how each of three contemporary philosophical points of view formulate consistent and coherent answers to the specific issues and questions presented in the last section. In our varied experience with public and private schools we have found people, institutions, and curricula that represent rather consistent commitment to the traditional or classical, the scientific or positivistic, and the transactive or interactive systems. Perhaps after you have read this set, you will be able to more readily identify your own values and commitments.

A. TRADITIONAL FORMULATIONS

CONCEPT OF MAN

Potential: Ability to Know "Truth"

The idealists believe that the world of man's experience is a phantasmagorical projection of the "real world of ideas." This universe of "truth" is absolute in its perfection and is available in part to those men who will learn to ignore the local circumstances of sensory information. Such men are capable of

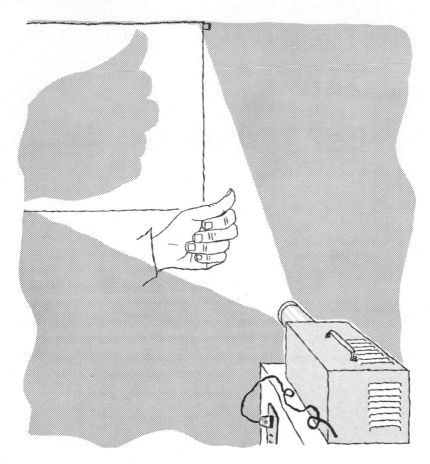

MAN'S EXPERIENCE AS A SOURCE OF TRUTH.

understanding more and more "universal ideas" and therefore are able to come to grips with more and more of what is "real" in the universe.

Each person is very incomplete and imperfect. But most of us, if we choose to study the right material in the right way, can learn more of what is true. Truth is the expression of the "absolute mind," which exists independently of and prior to the existence of the mind of any individual. Until we realize that we are incomplete expressions of "absolute mind" and truth, we naively accept the world as we see it. With careful study and analysis of man's best experiences, we can find a number of consistent "ideas" or basic truths that have been and always will be. In spite of the fact that we are born with limited ability to perceive the universe of ideas, with training and perseveration we can come to know at least some of the universe more clearly. The individual differences in potential that are of concern to the idealists are those that occur in the endowment of "mind." Reasoning and understanding are not associated with biological functions as some other philosophies and theories may hold.

This concept of man is best demonstrated in the kind of ultimate educational experience that is planned for him. For the traditionalist there is more ultimate truth and less distortion in the classical arts of philosophy, art, music, poetry, and mathematics than in the more applied science areas. Developing man's potential to the fullest requires careful construction of curriculum consistent with absolute truth and man's capacity to know truth. The ultimate goal of man is unchanging because the perfect world of ideas is complete and unchanging. The individual man is capable of changing from the narrow sensory-oriented person to the expanded mind that searches for and occasionally finds absolute truth and reality.

Morality: Consistency with "Absolute Truth"

This interpretation of reality assumes the existence of an absolute mind that is large, complete, and totally capable of comprehending the true world of ideas. Each human being with his small mind is a shadow of this more real absolute mind.

Morality is consistency with truth and reality. Only the absolute mind is capable of completely moral interpretations. Each human mind is a microscopic model of absolute mind; therefore, we can be moral only in part at birth. We are capable of increasing our moral thinking as we extend ourselves towards absolute mind and ultimate reality. The only deterrent would be inaction towards the realization of truth or denial of the truth discovered or made known.

Implicit or explicit support for this concept of morality is found in states, cities, schools, and departments that publish instructional guides and content directories for the use of teachers. The assumption here is not that teachers are stupid, but that those who have studied the content and methods of instruction over a longer period of time know more and better what the purposes of the school are than does the individual teacher or the learner. The teacher's expertise is in the interpretation of content to the learner, and the learner's expertise is in the ability to acquire knowledge.

Moral school administrators and content experts fulfill their obligations by devising a curriculum that is consistent with the best that is known and knowable. The moral teacher fulfills his obligation by teaching those things that have been selected and demonstrated as best. The student fulfills his moral obligation by diligently pursuing the educational tasks prescribed by those in authority.

Response Mode: Contemplation of "Reality"

Man in his search for absolutes is extremely limited in the ways and means available for him to study the universe and its truths. In his search for universal self and more absolute mind, his ends are fixed, but man himself can be very active and contemplative. Truth is there to be defined and experienced by the individual. The process of discovery is active, even though the end of the quest is fixed and unchanging.

The socratic method of verbal interplay is a penultimate process that encourages a rational investigation of reality. First, the questions are formulated by established authorities who know the universal truth. Second, the questions are ordered so that they logically lead to a predetermined and known answer and preclude illogical excursions into untruth. Third, the experience is kept at the rational verbal level, which minimizes the illusions of personal reality and emotionalism. By using such a method the natural response mode of man becomes the most "real" way of discovering the ultimate in knowledge. The only more perfect method of knowing truth is found in the contemplative thinking of the philosopher.

SOCIETY

Structure: Stabilized Institutions

All relationships involving individuals, classes, or institutions are most effective when they are stable. Harmony is promoted as stability is established and maintained in these relationships. Accordingly, when these conditions exist, there is no imperative to change the role of any of the elements in society. All segments of society support the predetermined plan for society, including its authority figures and the roles assigned to them, without feeling discontent or the need for change. Once balance and stability are achieved, the society in general requires no change (as long as no external forces operate to disturb the internal situation). All classes would tend to accept the status quo, since change would unbalance the social order.

One way to indicate the value of stabilized institutions in an educational system is to imagine what might happen if the structure of the elementary schools, secondary schools, and colleges were not maintained. Ponder an elementary school that would not assure us that youngsters would ever be taught to read. Suppose that simple arithmetic might or might not be included in the curriculum, and that training in writing was only an incidental study. Further complicate this educational chaos by imagining a high school which at any time might abandon its language or mathematics programs without cause.

Perhaps the best way to generate a sympathetic understanding of the value of a stabilized institution is to imagine yourself as the admitting officer at a college. You are trying to assess the potential of a student from the above-described system and his ability to succeed in your university. How would you make a judgment about the student if you had no way to assess his experiences or the educational institutions he had attended?

Authority: Assigned Roles

To maintain a society in the stable harmony described above, someone must have an assigned role of determining and insuring the orderly functioning of the society. Such persons or groups facilitate and oversee the maintenance of stability of the society for its own protection. This type of society is an efficient one to the extent that each function is assigned and carried out. Problems would arise if, for example, each person decided how to choose his role or carry it out. Gaps would result in the organizational life of the society. This would lead to serious impairment or breakdown of the society.

Education for a nation is a continuing process — one that does not start when a new teacher enters a system or cease when another retires. The decisions must be made in terms of the ultimate aims and purposes of man and society. Authority, if it is to further the knowledge of truth, must be a stable role in a stable society. Building principals or system superintendents cannot be expected to operate effectively if they are subject to a series of political or social campaigns to keep office. The authority of the principal comes from his ability to move the school toward its ultimate purposes, not from his ability to please the teachers he must supervise. The classroom teacher's authority comes from his responsibilities in instruction and not from the expectations of the students. The student's authority comes from his assigned role within the educational system and not from meeting the demands of his personal needs or the anticipations of his parents.

Mobility: Controlled and Restricted

Mobility must be restricted to maintain carefully defined and executed roles. Mobility as a process would deny the essential fixed relationships in society; that is, if a peasant could move "up" then a king could be moved "down" (or out). Such notions necessarily are not espoused in these systems! Change as a process is interpreted as a disruptive or a destructive force. The plan for society is complete and must be kept free of those elements that would reduce its inherent perfection. Stated more simply and positively: The good society must be protected from those who would change it by altering their place in it.

The conventional educational system operates under this particular mandate. Certification and tenure practices tend to restrict the kinds of mobility and define the ways by which a person may move up in the educational hierarchy. The requirements for moving from classroom teacher to supervisor are complicated. It takes extra years of professional training and a complete change of responsibility. Such modifications in role are not really encouraged except for the very rare individual. Retention and tenure policies do, however, provide security and support for those persons who fulfill their assigned roles effectively. All things considered, the system tends to produce people who find satisfaction in their work and would rather accept the rewards of their station than to strive to become a commissioner of education.

Communication: Prescribed

Communication has long been recognized as the vehicle of change. Therefore, this process has to be carefully restricted in societies that are not anxious to entertain changes. A king for example needs to communicate freely with some, but must be careful not to communicate with very many except on an official level. Each informed person can become a threat to the established system. Throughout history various groups have attempted to maintain closed or secret subsocieties. This was true of various groups of clerics, early merchants and craftsmen in their guilds, and various landed aristocracies. Even in closed societies communication is vital. Indeed, communication between king and peasant is so vital in fixed societies that prescribed and proscribed procedures have been developed. Ceremonial forms of petition, proclamations, and the utilization of intermediaries permit the various strata to remain in contact without fomenting change.

Responsibility: Predetermined Code

A teacher's responsibility by custom, tradition, and experience has been specified. Anyone entering the profession is

29

required to accept these codes and exercise them. Competing and conflicting roles as supportive mother, social worker, or psychologist are reserved for others not charged with teaching. If each teacher were to determine his own responsibility as a teacher some tasks might be done twice and others not at all, either course of action would detract from the validity of the student's education.

Obligation or responsibility is not a matter of personal conscience or group process, but rather a code of behavior dictated by the assigned function of each class of persons. The colorful, romantic code of the "Knights of the Round Table" serves to show how much an individual might be required to sacrifice as payment of his social debt for the privileges and responsibilities assigned to him.

Behavioral codes are predetermined. The source of this predeterminism may be, for example, a diety, a great man, or a good society as defined by a ruling class. Man's primary responsibility is acceptance of his status in life. If man were to doubt that all was determined by a force greater than himself he might have to question the validity of the social order and perhaps even attempt to institute social change.

Societal Ethics: Ends Justify Means

All means are justified by ends. Societal ends are determined by forces above man or at least beyond the common man. The ends generally are more important than any one man. Any man who contributes to the accomplishment of the ends of the society is a moral man. "Good means" are those that facilitate the "good ends" of a society. Therefore, a man is moral when he does anything that achieves the social ends. For example: political purges, holy wars, and genocide have all been "acceptable" means for attaining social ends in societies that otherwise have *not* accepted the notion that the killing of men is justifiable.

EDUCATION

Basic Objectives: Knowledge of "Truth"

The fundamental objective of education is to present the young with as much of the discovered truth (the operation of the absolute mind) as is known to man. A secondary purpose is to direct man to the areas of the human experience that are most likely to produce a recognition of absolute truth. New understandings are derived from the contemplative study of universal human affairs. These viable and enduring experiences are the most reliable projection of absolute truth and mind. Since the most effective perspective can be gained by studying human endeavor while it is not changing, the historical study of man provides the most fertile focus of inquiry.

Education is perceived as a specialized experience in the search for ultimate truth. Each individual is given an opportunity to be educated to the extent of his capacities. Those who are unable to profit from abstract studies are transferred to training programs and are taught the scientific and practical skills required to support the ideal society.

Goal Determination: Accord with "Absolute Truth"

The ultimate goal of education is, has been, and will always be the development of men who are more capable of acting in accord with the universal mind, that is, perceiving universal absolute truth. The design of education was fixed when the first man existed with an incomplete understanding of the universe. Education is a formal process of seeking universal truth. It varies from culture to culture only in the particulars of classroom organization and the conversational language used to communicate. These differences reflect man's imperfect knowledge of what should be. At some point, man's intellectual evolvement will move toward universal languages and uniform instructional programs.

31

FORMULATIONS

Since the goals of education are properly defined by the analysis of what we know to be the ends of education, the ultimate goal of mass education is the conservation of, not the experimental or empirical manipulation of, knowledge. Educational practices that cause learners to know and value truth are more important in public education than those that promote skill in testing truth. The discovery and validation of truth is a function apart, above, and beyond the capabilities of the average elementary and secondary student. But, in any case, the society will advance as more people become aware of and desirous of living in accord with truth.

Content Criteria: Reflection of Absolutes

All content that promotes the understanding of the absolute self, truth, and mind is valid. Since the physical sciences are but crude shadows of the real world of mind, and since the practical arts are even more distorted reflections of reality, these areas of study seldom promote any significant contribution to our knowledge of absolutes. The contemplative arts and the expressive arts, as expressions of man in his attempts to respond to or comprehend the ultimate dimensions of the universe, are much more valid than the sciences.

Such areas as mathematics, literature, and the fine arts are more likely to reflect the world of ideas than are the areas of physics, experimental psychology, or physical education.

Social Function: Perpetuation of Stable Society

The basic purpose of education is reflected directly in social function. Education as a process prepares people to know more of truth. It also prepares them to perpetuate the search for truth by providing a culture and a formal institution in which the quest is highly valued.

In the more perfect society of this type education is available for all to the extent that they can profit from a study of the universals and the absolutes. Since only occasionally some rare person makes a significant breakthrough (and then usually only the most educated and introspective individuals), the average person would be educated to appreciate and accept the universals found by others. Common man is also taught to accept the society that makes such discoveries and contemplative study possible and desirable.

In educational terms the social function of public education is to prepare each individual to find and fill a satisfying and socially worthwhile place in society. Satisfaction is essentially derived from the successful execution of an assigned role. The school can help by providing each child with an educational preparation commensurate with his abilities. The judicious use of a track system permits the school to serve each child more in accord with his ability and the opportunities that he is likely to experience. To the extent that the track system is effective, no one is over or undereducated. Further, no one need find himself unable to fulfill his social obligations nor will he be striving for roles that are beyond his capabilities.

Learner's Role: Active Acceptance

The ideal student is one who is critical in the sense that he expects his mentors to present logical statements and cases reflecting absolute truth. He is active in that he demands "proof" and rejects incompleteness or inaccuracies. He is accepting of truth when it is communicated within the framework he has been taught to recognize and value.

As developed above we would expect all but a few exceptional individuals to accept the educative processes and the educative institution exactly as they are presented. These institutions and practices are extensions of the absolutes that the most "aware" men of our times can derive. There is little need for the average man to contemplate changing education. It is possible that a truly great "thinker" may discover some more "truthful" way of educating the uneducated, but it would take a tremendously "in tune" individual to make a contribution more significant than those made by the scholars who have studied the universal experiences of man and discovered the basic principles of education as we know them.

Ultimate differences in the ability to experience reality are observed and accepted but not as a function of organic factors. The reality of man is expressed by his intercourse with ultimate truth and has little, if any, direct bearing on the biological phantasma of the brain or central nervous system. Differences in endowment do occur and are acknowledged in the good society, but only as they reflect man's ability to know the truth.

TECHNOLOGICAL FORMULATIONS

CONCEPT OF MAN

Potential: Comprehension of Natural Law

For the scientific realist, the physical world in which we live is the basic reality with all its parts behaving in some systematic organized fashion called natural law. Human action and all of nature is likened to an enormous machine operating according to mechanistic laws.

Man's evolution from the beginning of recorded history to the present time has been an orderly expression of natural law, which has taken him from a brute to a reasoning, intelligent creature. The use of his intelligence to study natural law enables him to understand his environment and to effect some changes in it.

Formal education as a public function designed for each according to his ability is an economical way of assuring that the entire population will have a chance to advance themselves and society as far as talent and motivation permit. What man will be a million years from now will still depend on how much knowledge of natural law he has and how well he applies what he has learned.

34

Morality: Harmony with Scientific Truth

Man is moral when he is natural. To follow nature is to accept the conditions that nature sets for existence and to abide by and bring oneself into a closer harmony or conformity with the laws of nature. Conforming to that which is real or natural is good and, hence, moral. For the realist, natural law relates to human behavior as well as to motion, time, heat, pressure, and other physical phenomena. For example, when we have studied the behavior of man and other animals under experimental conditions we have been able to derive some parts of natural laws and to make a few simple predictions of behavior. Until the present such experimentation has been limited primarily to basic physiological processes. However, the knowledge gained suggests that all of man's behavior is governed by natural law.

Physiologically moral men — those who live in accord with natural law — live longer and healthier lives. Moral societies also survive longer and operate more effectively than those that make no attempt to discover or implement natural laws relating to groups of men.

A perfect, healthy, and moral society is one in which man has "uncovered" all the moral laws of human behavior and is living in perfect conformity with all such laws. The moral teacher, therefore, is one who teaches what we know about the real world in accord with the natural law relating to the nature of the learner and the learning process. Truth as derived from experimental studies takes precedence over personally derived preferences in educational practice. The technologically oriented teacher does what he knows he should do even when it is in conflict with what he would like to do.

Response Mode: Complex Mechanical Reasoning

In a universe defined as mechanical in nature, man must react to the forces in the environment in the same way that a billiard ball must react to the decisive blow of a well-aimed cue.

35

FORMULATIONS

The response of the cue ball can be summed in terms of the forces applied to it from the outside. The realist interprets man's reactions in much the same fashion. But because man has a complex brain, he is not limited to an elementary reactive response. It is currently fashionable for realists to liken man's mental functions to a giant computer. The computer operates only on the basis of data fed into it. Man's intellectual behavior is also viewed as a function of the environmental forces that have been fed into him as a living organism. The impingement of these forces on man in particular patterns results in the shaping of behavior. Responses, although always mechanical and reactive, are complex and result in compounded interpretive and manipulative responses.

Recent advances in science and mathematics have facilitated the use of the mechanical model and computer analogy as the basis for the experimentation that challenges the conventional concept of the self-contained classroom and the usual role of the teacher. Computers programmed in extremely complex patterns are able to react to student responses with such specificity and relevance that it is not unusual for even very young children to "talk," "write," "listen," and "reason" with a computerized instructional device. CAI (computer-aided instruction) has already proven to be a successful auxiliary educational device. The usefulness of such an approach will depend on how compatible the basic assumptions of this technology are with natural law.

SOCIETY

Structure: Evolving Toward a Natural State

Social structure is subject to change toward specified goals through reasoned procedures. The primary purpose of social endeavor in a changing society is movement toward the reconciliation of social practice with "natural law." Specific goals and purposes once determined tend to be relatively consistent. Institutions are generally stable but are subject to revision when they fail to support movement toward the declared end.

In a modern, scientific, changing society institutions and

methods are evaluated through experimental analyses of results. "Fine tuning" of institutions in the sense of bringing them more closely in line with natural law must be accepted and promoted.

It is not entirely unreasonable to suggest that contemporary attitudes toward social unrest, especially on campuses, reflect a basic commitment to an "experimentally" oriented wait and watch attitude on the part of administrators, faculty, and the majority of nonactivist students. The underlying assumption seems to be that if the movements are good (natural) they will survive without intervention. If they are bad (unnatural) they will not survive. The realist apologists for the permissive climate see this as an opportunity to observe and evaluate a natural experiment in social evolution. Those techniques that produce viable change without active support will be assumed to be in accord with natural law. These will eventually be accepted, given support, and fostered by the educational establishment.

Authority: Competency in Science

Authority is derived from competency in the ability to uncover or implement natural law. Those who are seen as best facilitating societies' movement toward its goals are accepted as authorities (for example, astrophysicists and medical researchers). The hierarchy of authority consists of three groups: those who uncover natural law, those who apply natural law, and those who behave in accord with natural law.

Persons, groups, and institutions are assigned authority and responsibility to the extent that they contribute to the achievement of natural ends. Where the goals and ends of a changing culture are well defined, authority is accepted with fervor by individuals and groups. If the goals and ends are poorly defined, there will be passive acceptance or even rejection of authority, and the society will have to be regimented by the agents in power.

People are given the authority to execute responsibility in society by proving that they have competencies as evidenced by internships, supervision, and certification. Society regulates the authority it delegates to the practitioner by examining and certifying the adequacy of professional experiences and academic training. Physicians, attorneys, psychologists, engineers, architects, dentists, educators, nurses, veterinarians, real estate agents, and all others who consider themselves professionals accept the responsibility for proving themselves to be competent in their respective sciences. In turn they expect and receive social endorsement and the right to practice in their particular fields.

Mobility: Reward for Approved Behavior

For the realist, upward social mobility is delineated as a reward for approved behavior. Upward mobility is usually tied to increased responsibilities in one's relationship to the society. There is no particular thrust for development of social classes or for the maintenance of class structure. Those who promote the goals of the society receive social recognition (because they help to move the society toward ends previously specified as "good"); classes of a sort do develop. Thus, although some changing societies proclaim that "all men are equal," persons who emit more approved behavior tend to be rewarded with more favorable jobs, better living conditions, or other material or social benefits.

Upward mobility in the educational system is dependent in large part on the success record of the educator being considered for appointment to supervisory or administrative positions. Success is defined as efficiency in carrying out prescribed social functions. The basic assumption is that the person who best fulfills the responsibility of a limited educational role should be rewarded with the opportunity to meet the obligations of a broader assignment. The coach who has a winning season, the science teacher whose students won the most prizes in the county science fair, or the drama teacher who has produced a play that received state-wide recognition are logical contenders for an open principalship. The person freshly out of a graduate school of educational administration with superior credentials would have to offer other equivalent measures of educational success if he expects to compete with the teachers cited above.

Communication: Structured Process

Structured communication processes are determined through societal needs and goals in a changing society. Communication is necessary to facilitate the discovery and application of natural law. Government, education, and other information sources are committed to promoting all communications that move the society toward its ultimate social goals.

Communication proceeds laterally and vertically in the changing society. For example, scientists communicate with other scientific thinkers; they also communicate with practitioners and consumers of science such as educators and public figures.

In a properly functioning school mass meetings of the faculty as a vehicle of communication with administrators are generally frowned on. Seldom do spontaneous or emotional meetings result in lucid, rational statements or proposals. Most administrators in the public schools would find it unprofitable to meet with any but a group of people chosen for their ability to communicate the sentiments of the body they represent. By the same token, when school administrators feel compelled to petition the state education department, they too would be expected to meet in congress and first work out their differences. Their task would be to present a rational, concrete plan that could be assessed by the state superintendent of schools. Very few state superintendents would willingly accept an unscheduled and unstructured meeting with a group of uninstructed local administrators.

Responsibility: Function of Social Role

Individual obligations are a function of social role. Citizens are rewarded for acceptance of social roles that move the society toward "good" ends. Roles adopted by persons carry with them certain tasks and expectations that constitute obligations and responsibilities. Those citizens who perform their tasks acceptably are valued as responsible citizens. Persons who perform exceptionally are rewarded, in part, through recognition and, in part, through an opportunity to serve in even more responsible positions.

Individuals are important then by virtue of their service and contribution to the social ends. Roles exist as they serve the ends of the society. Each role mandates certain types of behaviors, which, when accepted, define a person as responsible. Behaviors that are deemed necessary for the movement of the group toward the "good" ends are rewarded. Those behaviors singled out by this natural selection process become part of the customs and mores of the society.

One example of an improper definition of responsibility in the educational framework is the person who honors a natural inclination to assume a "mothering" attitude toward students. In a "natural" school such a person would be required to assume another set of behaviors, which by common usage has become known as an "academic role." If the teacher is to really facilitate a knowledge of ultimate truth in the classroom both students and teacher must set aside the unrelated behavior of personal reaction and restrict their relationship to those behaviors that advance both parties toward a formal appreciation of knowledge. As insensitive as it sounds there are times when a teacher cannot and must not give up the professional role as teacher and assume the role of a supportive substitute mother or father.

Societal Ethics: Relevant Means Justified by Social Ends

All relevant means are justified by the social ends served. The social ends of a changing society are found in natural law. Ends are expressed as the dominant values of the society and its controlling agencies. Any relevant means, that is, those that can be shown to produce movement toward natural law, are valid. Means are not "good" or "bad," only valid or invalid.

Change in a realist society is not an end but rather a means of attaining some end. Such changes that do occur happen as the result of new discoveries and interpretations of natural law. Those changes that are proven to produce movement in the direction of "good" ends are validated and, therefore, are institutionalized.

A relatively new approach to the education of the profoundly retarded demonstrates how the means are justified by the ends achieved.

Behavior shaping, which is closely related to many traditional animal training programs, is highly repulsive to many observers who look only at the behavior of the moment and not at the end results. The idea of these "poor" children spending time learning to respond to stimuli beyond their comprehension by the use of food or drink reinforcements offends some who expect love and attention to work a miracle.

More than 50 years of ineffective training methods have generated a need for new knowledge of how these children learn and how we should teach them. These methods, so similar to animal training, have taught children to feed, bathe, and clothe themselves and to play, laugh, and talk when other methods have failed. Other than that behavior shaping has little to recommend it!

Realists who are concerned with teaching these children are enthusiastically testing and experimenting with the method of shaping and ignore those who do not like the mechanistic approach.

EDUCATION

Basic Objectives: Discovery and Application of Natural Law

The general objectives of education for the realists are the definition, refinement, and transmission of the culture. The ideal culture is defined by revealed natural law. The ideal transmission process (education) prepares the person to accept and fulfill a place in society. The ultimate social objectives of education are to facilitate the maximal discovery of natural laws and to bring the social order in tune with revealed law.

The school is an institution designed to promote inquiry about and application of natural law. The purpose of education for a relative few is to be trained in the methods of inquiry or research. Their basic content becomes the study of the natural law and the technology of researching.

For the vast majority the purpose of education is to be trained

41

to understand and use natural law when it is presented to them. Some will receive sensible training as effective consumers: learning to live in accord with the natural law of peace, health, and prosperity.

For another broad group education means preparation for the technical or training in the ability to use natural laws in the development of the material or social environment. Practicing physicians, surgeons, consulting psychologists, engineers, and skilled craftsmen and artisans of all sorts have as their purpose the direct application of known natural law to the betterment of man in society.

Each type of education is as worthwhile as the other and the effective society provides education for each according to his abilities.

Goal Determination: Obedience to Natural Law

Goals are determined by what is accepted as good. For the realist goodness is obeying natural laws. The moral man lives by the laws that nature sets. Therefore, the good goals are to discover the natural laws and to produce a means for continually refining the cultural design in conformity with discovered law. In modern scientific realism science is in the best position to set goals, since science is committed to uncovering the natural laws that govern the universe. Natural laws deal both with inorganic, nonliving and with organic, living, and social aspects of the universe. Objects, forces, and the laws governing them exist independent of the knower or behaver. The goals of a social group evolve, and the goals of education develop as depth and breadth of understanding of natural law occurs via scientific inquiry.

Objectivism in goal determination is essential for effective educational practice. Broad goals of education are preselected. Education is best when it results in maximization of living in the social system in accord with known natural law. Achievement of the basic goals can most efficiently be measured through careful testing of scholastic aptitude and academic achievement. Effective teaching and effective learning are both best understood in terms of objective assessment of movement toward specified lawful behaviors. Goals, then, are external to the persona of the learner and the teacher. The teacher who is effective has learned how to carefully manipulate the conditions in the student's environment so that growth can be indicated on teacher-made and standardized subject-matter tests. The learner has the responsibility to accept the goals as interpreted to him and to be as receptive and efficient as the effectiveness of the learning situation permits. He accepts the validity and social value of the objective assessment of his progress as an integral part of his becoming a more productive member of society.

Content Criteria: Congruence with Objective Reality

Realism assumes a real world of existence independent of our perceptions. This real world can be known through the methods of science. Learning about this objective reality provides all the essential guidelines for human behavior. The criteria for content determination is derived from this notion. Accordingly, content is knowledge — that is, knowledge of the universe in terms of that body of natural law that has been uncovered. Content also includes the method of discovery. The process of discovery from the realist's view is an orderly, rational, objective, analytical process that can be taught to a human being.

The method of operationalism is highly valued by most realists because it specifies a magnificently ordered method for the observer to see the universe without distorting it with his own perceptions. Operationalism specifies that only that which is overtly observable is open to investigation. This is a specialized form of positivism (the doctrine that science is limited to observed facts, and to what can be rigorously deduced from facts). Positivism is a favored interpretation of scientific method for the realists. There are other statements of scientific methods (for example, Dewey, Stanley, and others), but positivistic approaches and operationalism are generally what the realist means when he speaks of science.

When applied at the classroom level, positivism asserts that the highest priority content consists of the consideration of information that is well documented and that has been affirmed by sci-

A NONOPERATIONAL DEFINITION.

entific methodology. The study of Mars may be a very significant study in the fifth grade if the children are asked to understand and remember the verified information we have about this yet unexplored planet. Its position in our solar system and gravitational impact on the earth, its size and orbital pattern have been operationally defined and can be incorporated in the educational program of a school committed to a study of the order of the universe.

However, suppose the teacher moves the lesson to a discussion of the meaning, significance, or existence of the canals on Mars. Such lessons are semi-speculative at best because our objective evidence is so incomplete that it generates conflicting hypotheses about the same phenomenon. To introduce the very young and untrained to such speculation is at best a secondary function to be done, if at all, after the primary purposes of education have been met.

The only less valuable experience in relationship to the study of Mars would be to introduce the study of the entirely speculative. For example, "Do Martians, if they exist, have the technology to produce weapons or tools?" Since we have no objective evidence of animate life on Mars, all considerations of the qualities of that life can hardly have been said to promote a consideration of congruence with reality. One could with equal value initiate a study of the personal friendship patterns of marshmallows. Certainly there would be no less fantasy involved and we might at least be able to negate any hypotheses developed.

Social Function: Experimental Refinement of Society

A realist society functions in such a way as to cause the amassment of true knowledge. This can only occur through careful natural observation and analysis. Nature contains all the laws relating to a good society. Through careful experimentation, observation, and analysis of existing societies—both animal and human—we can develop the good society (that is, one that is in tune with natural law). For the modern realist, science is the foundation of culture. The social function of education is to imbue youth with the necessary knowledge and scientific tools to enable them to grow to fully participating membership in a social group committed to finding truth and prepared to bring the social order in tune with newly known natural laws.

For example, since there is no objective evidence to prove that there are differential maximum intelligence levels among various races, the realist educator would probably support such experiments as the busing of students in order to insure an amalgam of races in schools throughout a system. This type of experiment would be justified on the grounds that, lacking evidence of a genetic basis for intellectual variation among races, differential educational experiences might be hypothesized as contributing to the imbalance of I.Q. scores which exist. Again, through the carefully controlled racial mixing with concurrent intelligence and achievement testing the educational impact of this technique or any other can be assessed. Busing can be continued or discontinued on the basis of objective information about how it contributes to the improvement of I.Q. scores of all the racial groups involved.

Learner's Role: Reception of Knowledge

The student as a person who is learning to become scientific is involved and is motivated. The learner is a recipient of knowledge and method. The learner is not conceived of as being one who passively accepts, but neither is he a participant in the development of his educational program. At least not until and unless he becomes so well educated that he actually participates in finding or uncovering truth or natural law. Most students do not reach this point. They are active, but they are receivers of knowledge determined by external sources (that is, sources outside themselves). They are tested by scientific procedures such as standardized tests. The best of these devices are constructed by experts in the respective fields. This process receives a good deal of emphasis because the realist considers the transmission of factual knowledge or what we know of natural law to be the major business of education. The learner is not ready to independently assess and solve problems until he has mastered a large body of systematically presented knowledge.

Controlled studies of the learning process have supported the obvious interpretation that a child learns simple things before he learns complex things. If he fails to learn the simple lessons, then he is often unsuccessful with related complex problems.

Educational programs that take this natural interest and ability pattern into account present the child first with simple descriptive problems before going to the more complex descriptive.

An almost traditional science project is that of looking at and naming the parts of a plant as an early botany lesson. Some time later nearly every child is given the opportunity to open up a peanut or bean and "discover" the potential parts of a plant. This more complex but still descriptive experience moves the student to new types of questions that he is now ready to investigate. What will grow if he plants a bean? Why doesn't he get a watermelon? After complex descriptive activities he is ready to participate in simple analytical experiences such as finding out why a plant grown in the dark is a different color than one raised in full sunlight. Eventually if he is tutored and moved at the right pace he will be able to solve such complex questions as, "Why is it unprofitable to save the seeds from hybrid flowers if you wish to repeat a color or flower form?"

TRANSACTIONAL FORMULATIONS

CONCEPT OF MAN

Potential: Capacity for Social Interaction

Man is an organism capable of growth and change, who moves from the simple self centered to the complex "generous self" through an active involvement in a process of social interaction. Human capacity is essentially open ended. Man's potential for growth and development is limited only by his cortical capacity, which is so vast that science has been unable to estimate it with exactness. The Dewenian terms dependence and plasticity denote two vital traits in man's growing nature. They are positive forces in the growth process.

In order to clearly delineate the notion of dependence as positive, it is necessary to emphasize it as a primary relationship in which an aware organism recognizes problems that need to be solved and accepts the fact that others with different ideas may be able to help him achieve his own goals. Thus, dependence becomes a basic socialization process. It is by acknowledging a need for others that man grows in self development. The maturing man does not become independent in the isolated sense. An isolated independent man has aloof, private goals to be achieved without mutual involvement of others.

The maturing man becomes interdependent; he learns to share the social process of goal definition in addition to identifying personal goals. He moves from involving others in his goal achievement to participating in shared goal achievement. Since man constantly faces new problems he is always caught up in the process of becoming dependent in new areas while he is approximating interdependent relationships in other areas. Thus maturity is not the converse of immaturity.

A second major trait of man's developing nature is plasticity. Plasticity is the specific adaptability of an organism for growth. Adaptability is not a passive experience having a change made in, on, or by the organism as the result of a reaction to the environ-

47

ment or some experience. It is a transaction in which man is aware of his interaction with his environment. He must also actively evaluate his experiences and as a result often change his environment. He neither submits to nor resists his experiences but rather encompasses them and their relevance. Development of self is a continuous process as long as man maintains some degree of plasticity — the ability to change himself when he sees the need to do so.

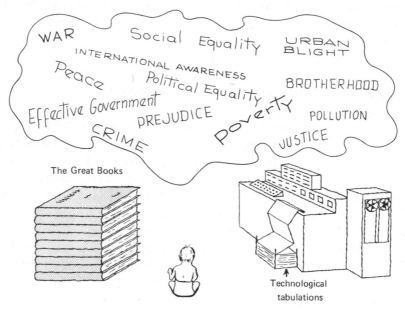

The Great Books

Technological tabulations

WILL EITHER SYSTEM FREE HIM TO HAVE A PERSONAL IMPACT?

Ideally, man never reaches a state where he does not need to grow. Man is not a fixed organism. His basic nature is to grow — not to "grow up" but to always be involved in a continuing process of more complex relationships. Transactions between the growing self and others are the essence of growth and ultimately produce greater potentialities in the self and in the society.

In practical terms a students potential is expressed as a function of his maturity. This use of the word does not imply that maturity is a state that will be achieved at some time in the future for the young or a state that was achieved by the old at some earlier time. The concept has no temporal dimensions. Social maturity is reflected in those situations in which a student can further his own ends while at the same time aiding and abetting others in accomplishing their ends.

Suppose that a teacher has been interacting with the other learners in the classroom and that the teacher has been effective in sensitizing the children to the personal and social advantages of interdependent behavior. Some measure of the potential or social maturity of the class could be inferred if the group were to plan and execute a surprise birthday party for their teacher. It would be no less mature for a second grade group to arrange for a menu of warm orange soda with peanut butter and crackers than for a high school group to arrange a pizza party at some local pizza parlor. The measure is in the awareness of the group for the basic humanness of their teacher and their own ability to offer a mutually satisfying experience without the direct aid, assistance, or insistence of the teacher. The transactional teacher in both cases would have a significant indication that the young people were realizing maturity appropriate to their life experiences.

Morality: Synonymous with Social Maturity

Moral behavior and social behavior are terms with many degrees of congruence. An experience that is not shared with others is not subject to social analysis or appraisal, and therefore cannot be considered a complete moral act.

Since men are born dependent and plastic as defined above, it follows that an immature person before social experience cannot be classified as a positive or negative force in a community. It also follows that the best description of the immature is that of neutral morality with a very great potentiality for growth and change. Since social interaction defines the nature of the moral experience of men, it follows that man is free only as he profits from knowledge gained through shared social experience. Man is always changing and growing—he is always becoming involved in more complex human relationships and, therefore, as a maturing person characterized as neither a good person with a good nature nor a bad person with a bad nature.

Standards of virtue separated from social transactions are not significant in this interpretation of morals and morality.

For the teacher, such a view of man implies that the learner be accepted for what he is. The teacher in so accepting takes into account the skills and talents of the student without judging him as mature or immature. Rather, the student is assumed to be an organism who has achieved a certain amount of growth with capacity for further growth given a meaningful environment for learning. The teacher makes the further assumption that the learner can accept some responsibility for himself. Thus he is expected to exhibit responsible behavior concerning those things that he has demonstrated he can do. A child is neither a miniature adult nor is he a capricious organism who operates with total disregard of those about him. He is a social being seeking expansion of self through interaction with others in responsible roles.

The kindergarten child who is engaging in social intercourse with teachers and with peers and in so doing uses "profane" speech patterns may be showing more evidence of transactive growth than the "nice" little girl from an upper-middle class home who purposely remains quiet or uncommunicative in her seat. The teacher would be entirely consistent with the frame of reference discussed here if he assessed the second child as being the more "disadvantaged" of the two.

Response Mode: Social Interaction

Man's response mode is best described as transactional, that is, man is interactive. Man is not a passive recipient of the environment—a blank tablet to be written on. Neither is he a mystical force that defies scientific study and description. Man is the consequence of a human organism being involved in a dynamic interaction with his environment. As the environment has potential to contribute to man's developmental processes, so too does man participate actively in modification of his environmental milieu. Such interaction is not to be conceived of as a dualistic separation of man from his environment. On the contrary, man is a system of systems—his identity comes from his relationships with other men and the many facets of his environment. He is not a collection of separate parts that function in mechanical unison. Means and ends are in continuity—inseparable. Growth of the mind depends on participation in mutual activities having a common purpose. All separations of mind from body, experience from thinking, or doing from knowing are false dichotomies.

A view of man's nature as passive—that man is reactive to the forces in the environment, that the role of man is to achieve some predetermined goal or level of maturity—is rejected. Instead, man is characterized by his involvement in initiating and interpreting his interactions with his physical and social environment.

The high school teacher who expects the classroom response mode to be a social and therefore interdependent interaction would expect if not encourage the students to challenge or demand proof of the most routine pronouncements made by the teacher. "Let's not forget who the teacher is here!" or "Where did you get your degree, young lady?" and other forms of emotional blackmail or academic intimidation would not be relevant responses.

The teacher might be more likely to ask the students to interview someone who holds a contrary point of view or better yet to invite that person to class. Each challenge to the teacher's point of view is seen as an opportunity to communicate and enlarge the view of the students and not as a hostile attempt to undermine the authority or authoritativeness of the instructor.

SOCIETY

Structure: Dynamic Process

The structure of a society is derived from the relationships of men in that society to one another, to the problems of the day, and to the shared goals and dominant values of that culture. Since all of these phases shift and change to some degree with the development of social and material advances, the structure of society grows and develops through an organic evolutionary process, which by its nature is unfixed and neither predesigned nor predetermined.

Fundamental questions of the 1970's are, "Do young people have a right to expect change?" and "Do they have a right to expect to participate significantly in that change?" The answer cannot be a simple yes or no.

Change for its own sake is rejected by this system. Only change that can be demonstrated to be relevant to personal and social problems at hand is mandated. If the ultimate goal of mankind is growth, then those changes that are required to facilitate growth make up the structural changes needed. The structure as it exists at a given time is that which we receive as our social legacy from earlier times and previous generations of men. Social structures that have undergone transactive development may be continually tested, but they are not assumed to be archaic simply because they were extant prior to our time.

All of us from the very young to the very old have the right to expect the privilege of social involvement. No person or group is considered expendable, obsolete, or inconsequential. Therefore, the involvement of the young in the ongoing process of social change is not only permitted but expected.

Authority: Social Endorsement

Authority is a societal endorsement of the social significance and general validity of the *authoritative* person in his areas of competency. Authority is not the privilege of forcing compliance with one's attitudes, values, or ideas.

The privileges of authority are those of being heard and having serious considerations given to the ideas expressed. The responsibilities of authority are in the self-imposed mandates to be authoritative in the information imparted and to be sincere in the interpretations and recommendations developed. In no case does this authority, which is delegated by society, imply the right of the authority to make arbitrary decisions regardless of the value or validity of the decisions.

The authority of the teacher or his right to permit or cooperate in the development of a transactive classroom comes from the fact that society has asked someone to accept the responsibility for involving the young in a series of critical educational experiences. Certification is a form of social endorsement. The certification of a teacher no more indicates the teacher is always right in what he is doing than does certification or licensure in the healing arts.

Society gives the professional person the right to practice or in a real sense to try, to learn, to change, and to try again to do a job that needs to be done. The right of the teacher to be transactive and to participate in the generation of transactive relationships comes from society's generalized consent to the development of experiences that will be helpful to a student in realizing his potential. Any classroom activity designed to promote the purposes of the society is authorized by the society. The authoritative teacher (one who knows how) is permitted and required to exercise his creative potential for the benefit of the students, himself, and society.

Mobility: Horizontal Movement Toward Complex Relationships

Social roles are expressions of the transactional relationships in which a person is involved. Each man has a variety of social interactions in a variety of shared social experiences. Roles are voluntarily selected and socially shared functions. They are not assigned, prescribed, or awarded by others.

Mobility is primarily a horizontal movement in which one extends himself to encompass more and more complex relationships with more and more people. There is no emphasis on vertical mobility since such mobility consists only of honorific corollaries of personal growth and development in some area of social significance. Vertical movement is not equated with "goodness." The "good" people and people of "honor" are those individuals who fulfill their chosen roles and perform their tasks with distinction.

The role of an academic department chairman serves well as

a hypothetical model of transactive mobility. The first assumption is that a person who has moved from instructor to administrator has been effective in whatever combination of teaching, researching, writing, and other forms of professional participation valued by the educational system in which he has been operating as a teacher. The second assumption is that his movement from instructor to administrator-instructor reflects his personal desire to enlarge the sphere of his professional impact. Academic elevations in a transactive system are neither a reward for superior teaching nor are they used as a way of removing the incompetent teacher from the classroom. Exciting interest in new instructional and in-service programs, promoting cooperative interdepartmental curriculum development, and stimulating concern for creative scheduling and staff utilization indicates the growing, changing interests of the person who is ready to move from the simpler individual responsibilities of teaching to the more complex, shared functions of education.

Communication: Shared Social Experience

Communication is essentially a shared social experience usually involving the spoken or written word. In a society that demands the participation of each member according to his experiences and insights, communication must be free and open. Unilaterality, regardless of whether it be between parent and child, teacher and pupil, or administrator and instructor, impedes the free flow of ideas and precludes the possibility of transactional process. Since each member of society is obligated to participate, he must be free to communicate.

The only essential restriction on the communicative process is to be found in the concept of relevance. If the speaker defines his terms outside the accepted patterns of usage, if he speaks of things that others have not or cannot experience, if he speaks of things that cannot be shared, then he does not speak to others at all.

The price of "free speech" is found in the individual's desire to speak honestly and openly to others about those things that he shares with them. If this happens then speaker and listener are involved and the likelihood of each having an impact on the other is increased.

If he can involve others by using language that has been shared, speaking about problems that can be experienced, in ways that do not violate the rights of others, his remarks are relevant and valued regardless of the extent of the agreement or the degree to which they can be implemented.

Many colleges invite students to participate as full voting members of departmental committees. If both the faculty and student members were transactive then far more often the pro and con divisions would be more fluid than they usually are. The expectation of a schism between faculty and student members is an example of a flagrant violation of the transactive mandate of sharing experiences. Less obvious to the average faculty member but just as insidious is the situation in which students always side with their "elders" or "betters." The most subtle nonshared, non-communication pattern found in college committees occurs when the students and some professed "radical" or "liberal" instructor form a fixed coalition against the "establishment." The sharing is more apparent than real if the sharing is a static nonevolving, nongrowing experience.

The committee in which the pro and con consists of different combinations of faculty and students on each vital issue probably reflects the most coherent transactional relationships of all those presented in this example.

Responsibility: Participatory Involvement and Growth

The individual is perceived as serving his own highest goals within a social framework and therefore his responsibility to himself is to increase the social dimensions of his own personality. We must note that this differs from several concepts in which the individual is subservient to the political or social order in which he finds himself.

The responsibility for his own growth and development can be accomplished only as he maintains some sort of participatory involvement in the growth and development of the social groups within which he operates. This is in sharp contrast to those anarchial concepts that advocate the freedom of the individual to operate outside of a social frame of reference.

There can be no arbitrary separation of man and society. An individual is a man only as he participates in society. Man is free to grow and develop through a process of social interaction within a given social and political framework. His responsibility is to promote his own growth via participation in the improvement of his society.

This same responsibility stated in terms of a simple social group is that each person must seek opportunities to serve his own ends better by improving the relationships he has with each of the members of that group.

Although one never quite reaches the point of taking responsibility for the actions of others if it means the sacrifice of his own integrity, one can reach a point where he will support another even though there be radical differences of opinion. The more one does for others and the more they grow and develop, the more social resources one has. Both the individual and the persons he relates to will become better people through shared social concern and behavior.

A transactive teacher assumes that provisional attempts to resolve problems on the part of the student will be almost inevitably accompanied by mistake making. Mistakes are not negative since they are an integral part of the testing, trying, growing process of which learning consists. The teacher is also aware that the involved and intrinsically motivated student will tend to accept the responsibility for correcting errors as he seeks a resolution of the problem he has encountered. Therefore, the teacher does not have to continually point out to the student what his responsibilities are or how the learner must meet his obligations.

Ethics: Relevant Means for Tentative Ends

If one believes that the ends justify the means then one will spend more time on the goals of education and worry far less about what happens on a day to day basis. If one believes the means justify the ends then one will search out the good things to do today and leave the long-range outcomes to fate, providence, chance, or God depending on the other dimensions of one's ethical frame of reference.

The transactionalists are unable to accept either of these opposing points of view and resolve the issue with their consistent interactive position.

The ends-means relationship is redefined with a rather unusual interpretation of the temporal and process functions.

First one does not work in the future or in the past. One does not do things because they need to be done in the past or because one wants them to be done in the future. The only significant dimension of time is the present and the present is always served in effective behavior. If one works in the present and has only this moment, then long-range goals serve only to direct one's present interpretation of present purposes. Since justification of what is being done is made within a social frame of reference, the behavior of this moment cannot be dominated by outcomes expected five years hence. Does it follow that the consequences of what we do not need should be of no concern? Transactionalists are not permitted the luxury of being personally capricious because they have defined the relevance of their behavior as being related to a specific social pattern. The pattern may change because of what is done, but there is enough consistency provided so that one is not licentiously free to behave today without regard for tomorrow.

Personal-social ends are dynamic processes incapable of becoming fixed and unchangeable. Ends grow from the behavior of people as expressions of their daily involvement in life. Ends can be stated only as the purposes for daily life and not as specific attainable products or completed states.

Consider the space exploration program in terms of means-ends relationships from a transactional point of view. Do the ends justify the means? Should the United States abandon all medical research to finance this program? Should we reduce our expenditures on public education to support this program? Should we sacrifice countless numbers of astronauts because we have to be first on some distant planet or should we declare war on the

U.S.S.R. to insure our sole exploration of the universe? These means have not been used even though they might have in some way furthered a specific static end of the United States being first or best at something.

Does this position assume that the ends are justified by the means? One cannot write history in advance but we have every reason to hope that all of the resources of America will not be invested in space when the mysteries of earth, the seas, our cities, the human mind, and peace on earth are beyond our grasp at the moment. Just because we might be able to do it does not provide justification for an all-out space program.

To be a transactive process our space program would have to meet all of the following criteria:

1. It would have to contribute to the improvement of man as he lives on earth today and not merely expand his knowledge of the universe.
2. It must have the active moral, social, political, and financial support of the main elements of the society.
3. The benefits of the exploration would have to be made available to all men of goodwill who are ready and able to utilize the information.

If the government adopted such a program for all it is worth to man instead of space at any cost or for the purpose of testing our technological toys, then we would expect the American public to continue its financial and political support of the program.

Ends and means are but the long and short view of what man is about. Any arbitrary separation will make man a slave of the past or the future or a victim of the present.

EDUCATION

Basic Objectives: Personal and Societal Growth

No introduction to transactionalists' concepts of education is complete without a statement of their predilection for process instead of product. The primary thrust of all curricular experience is to engender the learner's growing awareness of the personal relevance of his social behavior. The ultimate goal is for him to recognize himself as a personally and socially significant being. In recognition of this basic postulate the major concern is with the way things are happening and why they are happening. The end of an experience (the final outcome) is never as significant as the motivation and the process used. This posture avoids two positions, which are extremely undesirable.

First, people should not be overly concerned about end products because if they are then they may be satisfied with the product or final outcome with little consideration for the means used to achieve them. For example, if a hunter decides that he wishes to get a deer and getting the deer became the ultimate measure of his success in hunting then it would be equally appropriate for him to buy a deer from another hunter, to run down a deer in his car, to hunt at night with a light, or to kill the first deer he sees regardless of sex or season. Fortunately, most hunters agree that it is the process of hunting a deer that provides the satisfaction and not the acquisition of the dead carcass. This is not to suggest that the good hunter would ignore the carcass and leave the trophy rack in the woods, but it does imply that objects have little value except as indications or tokens of the processes involved in their attainment.

The validity of this analysis is expressed in the countless hours spent by the hunter in tracking his quarry, the fisherman's patient quest for an elusive fish, or the philosopher's persistent attempt to formulate a more precise statement of relationship. It is never only the value of what will be accomplished, but the inherent value of what is being done that is most important to him.

The educational process, which is an amalgam of both social and personal functions, cannot be arbitrarily separated or independently investigated as discrete functions of personal or social ends or means.

Society's reason for having an educational institution is to insure that it will always have a pool of human resource material to participate in the process of societal self-renewal. The process of self renewal is the essence of life. A living society of mortal men then can stay alive and grow only as the young mature into responsible participation in institutional processes.

FORMULATIONS

In society the individual's purpose is best stated by the functions he may learn to perform if he takes advantage of his educational-social opportunities.

1. He will change and grow as he identifies himself as a responsible person obligated to participate in the orderly process of renewing his society.
2. He will grow and change as his contributions are shared with the other participating members of society.
3. He will grow and change as he identifies through shared social evaluations the advantages and limitations of the culture in which he is involved.
4. He will grow and change as he is given and accepts the responsibility for initiating social change.
5. He will grow and change as he shares with others the privileges and responsibilities of participating in the renewal of society.

In an educational system designed to support an organismic society, learned behavior is neither predetermined nor accidental but rather a systematic utilization of the realized and unrealized capacities of the individual within a social interaction paradigm.

Goal Determination: Transactional Relevance

Since the objectives of education are related to dynamic instead of static or mechanical ends, we must understand goals as process facilitators. The universe is continually in process. Therefore, all goal determination is essentially transitory. Goals once achieved serve as springboards to new goals. Persons are formulating new goals as an integral operation of the process of moving toward those already extant. Hence, transactionalist educational goals emphasize a growing edge approach.

Many contemporary philosophers, physical scientists, and social scientists have suggested that the only thing that seems to be constant in the universe as we know it is that the future will be different. This is true from one end of the scientific spectrum of investigation to another, for example, from mutant genes to molar social relationships.

Let us extend our previous example of the hunter and see how his goals might effect his behavior if he were to use them as defined.

The first characteristic of an adequate goal is that it must grow out of an existing situation. It is not derived from some preconceived notion which is generated outside of the experience and people involved.

Let us suppose that the hunter had read a good book on hunting and became excited about hunting foxes. Let us also assume that he lives in a suburban area between two rather large cities. He also has only Sunday afternoons to hunt. The last recorded sighting of a fox was forty-three years ago last March. He could certainly identify a goal for himself as having a traditional English type fox hunt in which he collects the fox's brush as a trophy. However, we hope that the exaggerations in our example indicate how unlikely he is to accomplish his goal because of its evolvement out of a set of circumstances other than those in which the hunter finds himself.

A second characteristic of the goal must be flexibility and adaptability. Since the local conditions surrounding any learner change constantly and since our knowledge of conditions not yet experienced is so limited, our goals must be flexible so that we may bring our expectations and the situation as experienced into a more harmonious relationship. We have to be free to change our minds and to "roll with the punches." If our goals are fixed, our behaviors must become prescribed and we are no longer participating in the definition of the situation.

Let us rejoin our hunter who this time has made his goal more realistic because he has decided now to hunt rabbits on his neighbor's forty-acre farm; the rabbit season is open; he has a hunting license; and the reports are in that the rabbits are out in abundance. He has now come closer to meeting our first criterion because at least his goals have grown out of the local conditions and he should have a chance at attaining his goal. His goal now is to bag his legal limit of rabbits on Sunday afternoon. After a four-hour hike through the brush, he has sighted only one rabbit and it was out of range. If he holds to his original goal no matter how good it looked before he was in the field, he will have defined an impossible task for himself.

61

FORMULATIONS

An additional bit of information—the bird season was open, small game were legal. He did sight twenty-three squirrels, eight pheasants, and eleven quail. Still his afternoon was a failure—he did not shoot any rabbits. Most hunters, regardless of the extent of their formal training in educational philosophy, could suggest what was wrong with his goals and could tell him how he could have increased his opportunities for enjoying the afternoon.

To illustrate the third characteristic of a dynamic goal, let us again visit our hunter. This time he has reasonable expectations in terms of local circumstances and he will now be happy with any mixed bag that he can get. Just as he enters the woods two of his friends come along. The men have had an absolutely stupendous day of hunting and hold the legal limit of every game creature in season on this day. Since they both have to leave on an extended business trip in the morning they have no time to dress their bag and they do not want to waste it. After finding out our hunter is out after small game and that he is flexible in what he is after, they press the full possession limit of everything available on our friend. Without any effort on his part he has everything he set out to get. Or has he? He should be extremely pleased. He could never have such good luck on his own. If his goal was to catch game as he said it was then this has been a successful hunt. We suspect that even the most naive sports enthusiast will agree that our hunter may not be completely pleased with his day. Since he was primarily a sportsman and not a provider for hungry children, his goal was very incompletely stated when he cited some animal's body as his goal.

It is true that any goal can be suggested by some goal object or experience, but the goal is not the object, or the experience, but rather what we do in relationship to that object or experience. The object helps us to define what it is we wish to do, but it is not our end.

Our hunter could tell us about that. What he really wanted to do was to have some reason to be out of doors doing something that he felt was masculine, proving that he had stamina, that his advancing years had not dimmed his vision, that his years as an executive had not deprived him of his appreciation of nature, and that he could if he had to, trust his own skills to provide food for his family. The game in this instance was an effective device for helping the hunter direct his behavior so that he could involve himself in all these activities in one afternoon; but the game as dead animals given him by other people doing what he really wanted to do for himself, would probably have so little relevance that most hunters would have difficulty in accepting them if offered under these circumstances.

The third characteristic of an effective goal then is that instead of restricting us it directs our behavior so that we become free to accomplish our purposes. If our goals are stated as the achievement of ends or objects then we are restricted. If our goals are stated in terms of what we wish to experience in relationship to goal ends or objects, then we are free to accomplish our purposes in as many ways as flexible interpretation of our circumstances will permit.

Perhaps the hunter who is "going hunting" has a better chance of attaining a more meaningful experience than the man who wants a legal limit of dead animals.

Content Criteria: Opportunity for Personal-Social Growth

The demands of social experiences are the primary determiners of content. Neither a disciplined mind nor knowledge of the state of the physical universe serves as an adequate rationale for the determination of content.

When a teacher insists that addition facts must be mastered before a student can consider problems involving subtraction, the teacher is imposing his perceptions on the learner. The teacher, by insisting that step A must come before step B, may be interfering with the development of the very understanding that he wants to facilitate, namely that addition and subtraction processes are fundamentally interrelated.

As much as this violates transactional philosophy, so does the idea that it would be better for the students to unilaterally determine the content based on capricious psychological whim or philosophical fantasy. No reasonable determination of content can be made without the active shared evaluation of all the parties involved in the education program.

Let us use a curriculum decision to illustrate this principle.

63

Suppose a group of students make a demand for the inclusion of some specific content in the curriculum of a given school or college. How should the content be evaluated so that a sensible decision could be made about its support and development? Rather than using the threat of boycott or violence as the primary motivation for the swift and careful consideration of the demand, the students in this frame of reference would take it on themselves to document the personal significance and the social relevance of the content along with a careful assessment of the extent to which this content was being included in the curriculum. To do this the student might well enlist the aid of the professional educators who deal with the content so that the request would stand up to the scholarly inquiry it deserves. Other types of professional educators would be consulted to provide the supportive information that could indicate how the type of content taught in the manner recommended would achieve the personal and social purposes cited. To support the contention that social ends would be served by the revision, members of the community would have to be involved in an appraisal of the detrimental effect of the assumed curricular deficiency. Members of society with no investment in how the material is taught should assess and determine the social necessity of the proposed revision.

When this has been done this socially significant and personally relevant revision would be submitted to the faculty of the educational unit for appraisal. Not to decide whether the revision is significant or relevant but to assess its feasibility within the resources and responsibilities of the institution.

At this time the experts on content and method would investigate the most efficient ways of implementing the revision and balancing this off against the educational activities that would have to be modified or eliminated in order to add the revision to the general experience of the student. The administrators would have to take the report of the teaching faculty and document the ways and means of financing and supporting the revision within the system, as it exists, and where such an accommodation is not feasible they would have to determine how to change the institution so that it would be feasible. The lay public would again be involved by determining how financial and community support would be generated for the proposal—in some cases through legislative bodies and in other cases through local school boards.

Although such an orderly and probably slow process is not in keeping with the social responsibilities of each of the groups as they now define their roles, and although the many groups in society with their aggressive postures of attack and defense probably do not have confidence in each of the other groups, a similar procedure must be the eventual pattern unless society repeats an endless cycle of passing autocratic power from group to group.

Social Function: Enrichment of Self and Society

The primary social function of education is the increasing involvement of the individual in the social assessments of the day. Notice this is different from some of the more conventional concepts that education is designed to give the young the skills that they will need to solve their future problems. It is also different from the approaches that suggest that society will be best served if we have youngsters studying the problems of the past and the ways in which they were solved. Essentially, education is for the here and now, not for deference to the past and not for deferment until some unspecified future.

Education uses as its content problems and issues related to the life experience of the students. Its method is that of defining problems, collecting data, formulating solutions, applying solutions, appraising results, redefining problems, refining data, revising solutions, retesting solutions, and reappraising results in a continuing process of involvement in societal processes.

It is important to suggest that these societal processes are not "kiddie" problems. Although much of the curriculum may involve the child at the level of his immediate environmental sphere, the child is also an active participant in the world of his parents, his church, his social agencies, and his community. As society in its many aspects is interactive, then all of the adult world in some fashion impinges on the world of the child. All of these impingements, from traffic rules to drug control laws, are a part of the child's universe and reasonable grist for the mill of education for social involvement.

This approach intends more than mere exposure to a broader set of stimuli than a person might encounter without formal education. Such an approach would not be nearly enough for a transactionalist. A maximal educational opportunity must provide not only an opportunity to receive information from broader social groups, but must permit him to be an interactive participant in the resolution of broader problems with a variety of people. Transactionalists do not propose to validate a hierarchy of persons for educational purposes. The child who exhibits exceptional intellectual ability is valued no more and no less than any other child who is fulfilling his social roles to his capacity. A course in auto mechanics is inherently no more or no less valuable than a college preparatory course in physics. Both may be more valuable or less valuable on the basis of relevance for living and adequacy for meeting social and personal needs of different individuals.

Learner's Role: Responsible Participant

The learner is a participant involved in the process of inquiry. The learner is not passive, nor is he a mere recipient of knowledge. Since the individual has intrinsic value as a person, regardless of age or social function, his social interaction is valued in this kind of educational philosophy. If meaning is assumed to be derived through social intercourse and through sharing common activities and common goals, then man cannot be independent or apart and still be a truly effective member of the society. It is only to the extent that man shares needs, goals, purposes, and ideas that these have meaning and provide a framework for an integrative society. It is only through such processes that a common core of the culture can be sufficiently developed to provide a foundation for man to live in true community with other men. The role of the learner then is to participate in the social medium of the school in order to develop and maintain an adequate self. A learner is one who can communicate, develop, share, and act on mutual needs and purposes.

It is not enough for the learner to independently or passively partake of the educational experiences someone else has prepared for him. At best in that kind of situation he can only have a limited involvement. A full, rich social interaction process, such as involvement in curriculum development and assessment of learning experiences, is necessary if the student is to have an intrinsically meaningful experience.

In summary, the transactional student would be more likely to respond to the teacher's attempt to provide a provocative environment for the student to experience by indicating, "Of all the things you have suggested and of which I am aware, I believe I should start my inquiry here on this particular problem. Will you help me when I need you?" Neither the often heard, "Teach me! It's your job" nor seldom heard but often expressed, "I will learn everything you ask me to" are indicative of responsible participation.

PRIMARY SOURCES FOR FURTHER READING

Traditional Formulations

Hutchins, Robert M. *The Conflict in Education.* New York: Harper, 1953.
Kant, Immanuel. *The Fundamental Principles of the Metaphysics of Ethics.* New York: Appleton-Century, 1938.
Plato. *The Republic.* Vol. 1, Cambridge: Harvard University Press, 1930.
Plato. *The Republic.* Vol. 2. Cambridge: Harvard University Press, 1930.

Technological Formulations

Bestor, Arthur. *Educational Wastelands.* Urbana, Illinois: University of Illinois Press, 1953.
Bridgman, P. W. *Reflections of a Physicist.* New York: Philosophical Library, 1950.
Council for Basic Education. *The Case for Basic Education: A Program of Aims for Public Schools.* Boston: Atlantic–Little, Brown, 1959.

FORMULATIONS

Rickover, Hyman. *Education and Freedom.* New York: E. P. Dutton, 1959.

Transactional Formulations

Bayles, Ernest E. *Pragmatism in Education.* New York: Harper, 1966.

Brameld, Theodore. *Toward a Reconstructed Philosophy of Education.* New York: Dryden Press, 1956.

Bruner, Jerome. *On Knowing: Essays for the Left Hand.* New York: Athenium, 1956.

Dewey, John. *Democracy and Education.* New York: Macmillan, 1916.

Childs, John L. *Education and Morals.* New York: Appleton-Century-Crofts, 1950.

SET THREE

Sciences and Systems

Earlier we briefly described education as it relates to the nature of man and society from three philosophical points of view. In effect, these descriptions state what education can do with and for young people and society.

We have found that most of the students of education who have had conventional instruction in the educational philosophies are able to recite detailed information about a wide variety of philosophical positions, but rarely are skilled in the use of this material in the evaluation of existing practice or in the development of new or improved approaches. This is basically because of professors of education and psychology who usually emphasize either the philosophy or the art of education. The methods professor who spends time giving to or demanding of the students the philosophical bases of educational practice is as unique as the philosophy instructor who feels valid evaluation of his course is based on the students' ability to extrapolate philosophy to the development or analysis of curricular or instructional practices. Equally true, students who have "passed" required psychology courses seldom are able to perceive a direct relationship between academic psychology and educational practice. The psychology professor usually presents the experimental or theoretical information relating to the learning process without involving the students in the educational implications of the material.

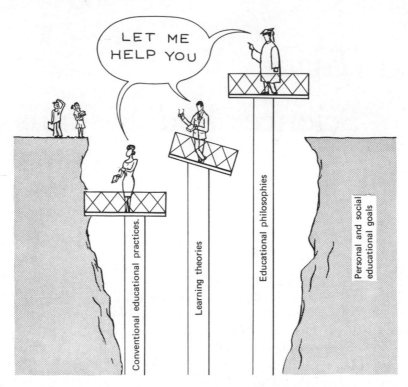

CAN THEY DO THE JOB INDEPENDENTLY?

Since everyone and, therefore, no one is responsible for this fractionation of experience for the student of education we shall stop throwing bricks from the balcony of our glass house. Instead we shall state what we believe to be a more agreeable juxtaposition of the components of professional preparation.

The fundamental starting point for the educator should be his educational philosophy, which tells him why he is educating and what should happen as a result of the educational experience. The methodology of instruction should be predicated on two logical bases—the purpose of education and the nature of the learning process. It appears logical to study the learning process of the child before we determine how we shall teach him.

Psychology today consists of a number of schools or systems (including mini-systems and nonsystem systems) that choose to use different levels of description and a variety of philosophical

70

assumptions. It is the latter that causes the sometimes bewildering array of learning theories and apparently conflicting evidence about the learning process. Until a unified philosophy of education is generated and until an all-encompassing theory or model of learning is accepted by psychologists, we can expect the student of education to continue to face the dilemma of whether to integrate his philosophy of education, his theory of learning, and his educational practice from his fragmented professional training or to abandon all hope and do what he is told to do or what he has seen done.

Since the task of divining the complete learning theory or model seems to be beyond the capabilities of the great psychologists of the day, we shall, in modesty, refrain from revealing it at this time. Instead we shall assay a limited number of theories that purport to present a systematic view of learning that may have significance for the classroom instructor.

THE CRITICAL ISSUES IN LEARNING

There are five basic questions that we wish to raise about the learning process that have a direct bearing on the teacher's behavior while he is trying to promote learning regardless of the philosophical ends of the educational experience.

TIME

When does learning take place? This issue is of paramount importance in determining the management procedures in the classroom. Suppose you have just completed a lesson concerning the development of a plant. Also assume that John can now answer your questions. If this is a measure of learning when did it take place? Did he learn when you used the film strip? Was it your lecture material? Perhaps his independent reading in the library? Did it occur immediately? All at once? Or was it a gradual process? For John it may not make too much difference since the most harmful thing that may have happened is that you have wasted some of his time by having him continue in "learning" activities after he has learned.

71

Now let us consider Wilma who failed to answer your questions. If we believe that this means she has not learned and if learning occurs immediately after the teacher does something, then she will not be able to learn unless the teacher does something else.

If learning occurs as a result of Wilma's doing something and she has not done it yet, then all you have to do is to get her to do whatever it is that she should do immediately before learning takes place.

Suppose for a moment that learning takes place some time after your presentation or Wilma's participation. In this case, it would not be wise to put too much emphasis on your questions that she could not answer nor would it be appropriate to make this early evaluation the only specific evaluation of her learning.

In essence, the issue of when a person learns is vital to whether you or the student should do more or less, when either or both of you should do it, and for the proper timing of evaluation experiences.

It is not at all uncommon to hear teachers say, "The lesson is over, I have done all I can do. We shall have to go on!" It would be reassuring to know for sure that the time for learning has come and gone before we leave a child behind.

CONDITIONS

How does learning take place? For the past decade we have heard singularly similar statements when we asked senior education students this question. Most frequently the response is, "Learning takes place when the teacher does a good job of teaching." Aside from the fact that we probably disagree with the implications of this statement, it does not say what learning is or what makes it happen. There are times when such extreme importance is attached to the teaching process rather than the learning process that one wonders if the implicit statement is not, "I haven't any idea of how somebody learns. But if I am lucky and teach as I was told, or as I have seen it done the bright ones will learn because of or in spite of me. The dull ones don't learn for anybody else anyway."

It is obvious that if we do not understand how learning takes place we shall have very imperfect notions of what we are doing right or what might be even more effective in promoting learning.

There are a number of interpretations of how learning takes place. They do not have equal and scientific validation. However, the teacher who utilizes a systematic viewpoint to analyze his teaching and the students' learning can better assess and modify his formal instructional program. He will have defined what learning is and how it occurs. He will be able to judge how what he has or has not done has caused or not caused learning to happen. He will have some specific systematic points to consider in the evaluation of his teaching behavior and the learning behavior of the students.

REASONS

Why does learning take place? Gold stars, honor clubs, good grades, teacher praise, opportunity for discovery, problem solving, carefully controlled presentations, ambiguous involvement! All of these and a thousand other things have been touted as the factors that cause learning. In any educational system that specifies learning is not accidental there is an implicit assumption that something causes learning or that learning is at least related to some set of conditions or experiences.

If there is a more persistent question than, "Why doesn't he learn?" it must be, "What can I do to make or help him learn?" In both questions, teachers are asking a basic question: What is the prime mover or motivator that causes or permits learning to take place? Professional journals and teachers' magazines are filled with things that have worked for some teacher some time with some group under some specific set of conditions.

The important issue for the teacher of a specific group is not so much, "what worked" but rather, "why it caused learning." If you can answer that question, you can vary the content and technique to fit your personality and the aptitudes of the children you teach. You will be able to develop your own materials and techniques with more confidence if you know which dimensions of the experience are essential to learning.

73

ACTIONS

What does the learner do when he learns? Such practical problems as the effective use of educational television, motion pictures, field trips, programmed instructional devices, lecture material, and laboratory experiences are directly related to what one believes the learner's roles and actions are in the learning process.

For example, if we believe that the learner is passive and responds to what is done to him, it might be relatively unimportant that he have an opportunity to function in a laboratory situation solving unique problems, which he generates.

However, if we assume the learner is active and responsible for his own learning to a large extent, then it might be a disaster to have a learning experience consist of a series of carefully controlled and directed recitation periods.

On the contemporary scene in higher education the confrontation regarding student government, student involvement in curricular and instructional policy making and implementation, may well be expressions of what the "establishment" and the "students" believe the role of the learner should be in a life experience that is at least nominally labeled as a learning experience.

OUTCOMES

How do we know when a person has learned? For more than seventy years, a growing body of information on experimental learning has been accruing. For most of this time there has been much debate over what is the most valid measure of learning. Teachers have also followed this development as reflected in the various fads and fancies in educational evaluation. To illustrate the problem in oversimplified dichotomy, which of the following is a more valid indication of learning: A wrong answer derived with a "right" method or a right answer derived with a "wrong" method? The relative merits of process and product as the more valid outcome in education have engaged the recognized authorities in philosophy and science and are still open to so much qualification that the professional literature for teachers continues to reflect ambiguity and equivocation.

A lively discussion of the merits of multiple choice, true-false, short answer, and essay questions is generated on the average every four-and-a-half minutes in a teachers' lounge somewhere in the United States.

Imagine what would happen if someone were to break in to one of these endless discussions and insist that we present our evidence that tests do measure the learning that has taken place. Angels would weep, administrators would wail, teachers would blanch with fear and professors of education would fulminate with righteous indignation, but what evidence would be cited?

There seems to be no other area in American education that has been subjected to such a professional indifference and academic sterility as that of ascertaining the validity of our assumptions about how we know when a person has learned.

THE TENTATIVE INTERPRETATIONS

As suggested earlier, each learning theory concerns itself with a different level of description of the learning process. Edward L. Thorndike chose to analyze behavior into very small units and to explain learning as the building of complex behavior through a process of accumulation. Two simple bits of behavior, when put together, form a more complex behavior. Thorndike felt that all complex behaviors could be understood as a fusion of simple units of behavior.

He described the basic learning pattern as a mechanistic response to external forces (in his language — rewards). A stimulus evokes a response. If that response is rewarded, it is learned. This is indicated by the fact that if the stimulus is presented again, the rewarded response is more likely to occur than any other.

B. F. Skinner, who follows Thorndike in chronological order, accepts some of Thorndike's working ideas. For example, they agree that complex behavior is really simple behaviors occurring in combination. Skinner agrees that the learning behavior is a

75

mechanical response to external forces. Skinner does not accept the importance of the original stimulus. He starts with a response when it occurs, no matter how it was evoked, and makes that response more likely to occur by the immediate application of reinforcements. Reinforcers act in much the same way as rewards do for Thorndike.

Skinner disagrees with the Thorndike position on the importance of the management of stimuli that come before a response. He is much more concerned with managing the reinforcers that occur with or after a response.

As you can probably begin to see the teacher who uses Thorndike as a learning theory model will be working in a different way from one who is using a Skinnerian approach. Such choices as using or not using a known stimulus will have a tremendous impact on the methods of teaching, as we shall see when we develop each theory in more detail.

There are many differences between these two positions that fall into the same school of thought, that is, associationism. One can begin to imagine how differently one might teach if he accepts the point of view of some psychologist with a radically different interpretation of learning.

The field theorists believe that learning occurs as a result of perceptual cognitive processes instead of the more mechanical associative processes referred to above. These theorists assume that people are able to think and to perceive and respond to a situation in accord with their perceptions and interpretations of a situation. According to these theorists people become involved in learning, and learn because of involvement at the personal-perceptual level.

Learning is not an inductive process. One does not learn what two is and then learn to add two and two to get four but, rather, learning is a problem-solving process of identifying four and the concept of fourness, what four is, what makes four, and how one uses four to solve problems.

As you can probably guess, both an elementary mathematics lesson and a college calculus class would be markedly different in orientation if the learners were presented with the whole problem first instead of at the end of a series of sequential experiences. For the field theorist, the whole is always more than the sum of the parts and cannot be inductively arrived at by adding part to part.

Specific behavior is not learned because some outside agent brings force to bear on the learning experience. Learning is a perceptual process of organizing relationships that we discover as we are involved in solving problems that have a personal meaning to us.

Just about the time that we apparently have agreement, we find with a little further analysis critical differences between those theorists who fit into this same general school of thought.

The Gestaltists believe learning proceeds from the whole to the parts. The phenomenologists, as represented by Snygg and Combs, believe that instead of discovering parts we really understand the whole in a more detailed fashion without ever really breaking the whole down into parts.

The Gestaltists are also concerned with learning as the organization of perceptions of the world outside the learner. Their interest in the individual is related to his perceptual equipment and mode of response. The phenomenological psychologists on the other hand take a very personalistic posture and suggest that learning is a process of discovering one's own relationship to the subject matter. The really important outcome is not an understanding of the complex relationships in history, as the Gestaltists would state, but rather the perception of one's self as a historian, that is, to know what history is and how it can be used to improve an individual's own conditions as he perceives them.

This difference separates the Gestaltist who would take the whole of history and make the study one type of cognitive process and the phenomenologist who would have the individual study history as a personal-perceptual process of determining means to solve present problems.

As you read the following sections and decide which, if any, of these points of view are most relevant for you, take into account the different levels of description involved and their impact on the logical development of sequential ideas.

Theories differ far more than they disagree. If two theories are describing different things differently they may be in basic agreement. Two different positions have to be taken on the same issue before they can be defined as being in basic disagreement.

The thrust of arguments A and B are not in opposition, since the same issue is not being dealt with by both. It would be extremely disputatious to reason that they were or had to be in disagreement.

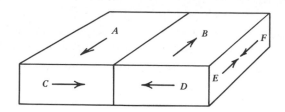

Positions C and D assume only analogous relationships. Although they might well be associated with related concepts that are in disagreement, any assumptions made about C and D are as imperfect as the analogy itself. Constructs E and F, on the other hand, are defined by the diagram as being diametrically opposed to each other in the same plane and within the same physical limitations. In this case, there is disagreement and one can honor only one formulation or the other depending on which is more consistent with one's frame of reference.

Many educational practices differ because of the predilection of one system for one activity over another. This preference for an approach does not mean that others are wrong or inconsistent with the theory in question. For example, the phenomenological system suggests a preference for a student's personal involvement with discovery as a highly relevant experience. Does this mean that a formal lecture prepared by the instructor has no place in this system? A simplistic agreement would run that since discovery is preferred then all but personal discovery is "wrong." Nothing could be further from the truth. Many types of activities lead to "personal" discovery.

All theoretical systems are imperfect and fail to describe all types of learning with equal validity. Theories are useful not because they answer all questions or indicate the correct way to manage all learning situations, but because they do a reasonable job of organizing the vast amount of experimental and empirical information about the learning process. They do provide a relatively consistent and functional frame of reference for an educational practitioner to use in the assessment of the consistency and effectiveness of teaching.

If you expect more of the theories you will be disappointed; if you demand less of them than this you may be investing your time in a professionally irrelevant activity.

THE CONSTRUCTIONS: LEARNING MODELS

The overall design and significance of conceptualizations of learning are reflected in the positions taken on key issues. We have chosen the following questions because of their face validity and relevance for the professional practitioner of education: What motivates a man to learn? What is the nature of the learning process? What can be done to promote learning? What limits the extent of learning? What limits the usefulness of what is learned? What determines the permanence of learning? To the extent that the questions are relevant and the exposition clear, fundamental similarities and differences should appear.

THORNDIKE

For nearly a half century the theory and research of Edward L. Thorndike's connectionism was a dominant force in psychology. In view of this preeminence it is not surprising that many texts in educational psychology as well as school books on reading, English, arithmetic, science (indeed virtually every common school subject area) reflected Thorndike's orientation.

The twentieth century has been an age of science. Thorndike provided educators with a scientific approach to formal learning, that is, an approach based on experimental research.

Many who use Thorndike-oriented materials are only vaguely aware of Thorndike or of the theory that he exposed. But because the materials and techniques are Thorndikian, the impact is

SCIENCES AND SYSTEMS

there. In Thorndike's connectionist theory, then, we have the first approach to pedagogy that was not founded in some pre-scientific armchair psychology or philosophy. Connectionism today continues to have influence on educational practice.

Motivation via Reward

First let us consider Thorndike's position on motivation. He viewed learning as an essentially reactive process. That is, the learning organism reacts to or responds to forces in the environment that are applied to it. Man in this frame of reference is seen as basically a passive receiver who reacts to stimuli in the external environment. Although Thorndike admitted the operation of innate factors in behavior, he did not study nativistic tendencies in his research. Motivation is caused by external instead of internal forces.

For Thorndike the basis of motivation was reward. The reward or satisfying state that follows a desired response serves to strengthen the connections or bonds between stimuli and responses. An organism, be it a cat or a man, will tend to repeat those responses that are rewarded. Thus an organism is largely externally manipulated by the differential effects of reward or lack of reward.

The way to obtain desired behavior in a student is to deliver rewards in sufficient quantity when appropriate responses are made. The strength of S-R bonds is thus effectively increased. Rewards must occur soon after the behaving and they should be an integral part of the teaching-learning act. Such rewarding increases motivation in the student, since it occurs in close proximity to the newly acquired behavior. Paying children for good grades earned at the end of a marking period is probably rewarding. However, it rewards the earning of the grade rather than the acquisition of knowledge. Hence this practice, although quite common among today's parents, does not serve to promote classroom learning. Rewards this far removed do not serve to effectively strengthen day to day learning. It neither rewards a specifically desired learning nor does it follow closely enough to any classroom responses to be maximally efficient.

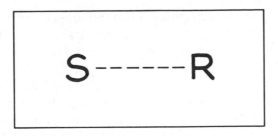

Fig. 1. WEAK CONNECTION BETWEEN A STIMULUS AND AN
UNREWARDED RESPONSE.

Learning as Connecting

The nature of learning for Thorndike was essentially the
strengthening of a connection between a stimulus and a response.
When an organism makes a response in the presence of a stimulus situation a connection is made (see Figure 1). As we have indicated by the broken line between the S and the R, only a mini-
mal amount of learning or connecting occurs in the absence of
reward. If the stimulus were presented again almost any other
response might be made due to the lack of reward in the previous
instance.

When followed by a reward, the connection between a stimulus and a response is increased (see Figure 2).

Then, when the same stimulus is presented again, the learned
or connected response is more likely to occur than unrewarded
responses.

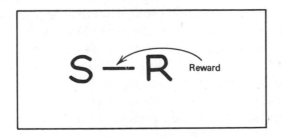

Fig. 2. A REWARD STRENGTHENS A CONNECTION.

In his earlier theorizing, Thorndike believed that punishment had an effect equal and opposite to reward. He theorized that punished responses were stamped out. Over the years Thorndike conducted numerous experiments on the effects of rewards and punishments. This work subsequently led him to state that, although rewards strengthened connections between stimuli and responses, punishment did not have an equal and opposite effect. Rather, Thorndike concluded, punishers temporarily stopped a behavior and provided opportunity for other responses to be made and rewarded.

Also, in his earlier work Thorndike wrote that exercise or drill caused a desired habit to be "stamped in," while responses not practiced were eliminated or "stamped out." Later the position on exercise or drill was modified. He suggested that exercise was important only insofar as it allowed reward to operate. He held that unrewarded drill or practice in the absence of reward was of little use. Controlled practice on the other hand, where reward operates when correct responses are made, does produce stronger connections.

Facilitation by Management of Reward

In his basic text on educational psychology, Thorndike noted that management of the learning situation such as exists in the classroom was more complex than the management of learning in the laboratory. Among the variables that are more difficult to identify are the specification of the bonds to be made or broken, the identification of those states of affairs that satisfy or annoy the learner, and the most appropriate way of applying rewards.

In organizing a learning environment it is essential that both teacher and learner know the characteristics of a good performance. Controlled practice with selective reward must be arranged. Errors must be quickly picked up and diagnosed so that they will not be rewarded and thus strengthened.

It may be observed that the teacher is seen as managing the learning situation rather completely. One is not primarily concerned with the internal states of the organism, but instead with structuring the situation so that rewards will operate to strengthen desired responses. The learner should be interested, problem oriented, and attentive. However, the best way to obtain these conditions is to manipulate the learning situation so that the learner accepts the problem posed because of the rewards involved. Learning proceeds from the simple to the complex. Attention is maintained and appropriate stimulus-response bonds or connections are strengthened through the precise application of rewards for interest, attention, and productivity toward the goals set by the teacher. A teacher's role is to cause appropriate S-R bonds to be built up in the learner's behavior repertoire.

A rather strict interpretation of Thorndike's management of reward would suggest the basic inadequacy of some conventional educational practices. One of the most obvious is the use of formal testing and the handling of related grades.

Most teachers will test at regularly scheduled times such as once a week or at the end of a unit or, even worse, once at mid-semester and once at final examination time. If one is truly looking for an opportunity to give rewards in order to strengthen the learning that has taken place, then the teacher should test very soon after the original learning. Too often conventional testing appears to the learner to be a cat and mouse game played by the teacher whose sole purpose is to prove that the learner has not learned or has forgotten what was learned. Forcing learners to save up for big examinations logically does support such a supposition. The learner inherently assumes that testing in such large "chunks" is not done to improve his learning. What may well be an unexamined practice based on the convenience of the teacher does increase the anxiety of the average pupil and probably decreases his overall performance. It also reduces his opportunity to earn the rewards he needs to really consolidate the educational gains that he has made.

The teacher should test frequently at logical points. The tests should be designed to offer students the opportunity for maximal reward. Test results and/or grades (rewards) should be made available at the earliest possible moment if they are to be most effective. Tests that can be machine scored can be made available to students in a matter of minutes or hours by the teacher who understands the necessity of immediate reward.

The prospect of a class looking forward to a test and eagerly anticipating the results would in most instances be a revolutionary attitude and behavior. Yet this is what Thorndike wrote in the 1930s and it was the only result he expected from the proper management of rewards.

Biological Limits of Connecting Systems

For Thorndike the difference between the bright and the not-so-bright was the number of S-R bonds available to the organism. Thus, intelligence is primarily quantitative.

To a large extent, the number of S-R bonds that an organism can make determines capacity. Once an organism reaches physiologic maturation neural structure changes little and thus capacity becomes relatively fixed. The most effective way to utilize the capacity of the organism is to build up the greatest possible combinations of connections or S-R bonds. A person with a greater repertoire is more intelligent, since he has more bonds at his command to use in solving new problems.

The relationship between bonds and intelligence can be clearly seen in the exceptional case of localized brain damage. Assume that a particular trauma makes our subject entirely unable to read the written word. A person with this particular disorder might well make as many connections as anyone else in listening activities or physical skills. His unintelligent behavior in reading is due to the fact that he is unable to make enough connections. Although there are many other variables that interfere with a person's ability to make connections biological limitations are almost impossible to compensate for. The teacher in such cases must use specialized instructional techniques that will permit the child to make as many connections as possible instead of trying to enlarge his capacity. Fortunately nearly everyone can learn a little more if the teacher is careful in the management of stimuli and rewards.

84

Transfer of Identical and Similar Elements

How does transfer occur and what limits are there on the transfer of what has been previously learned? Elements learned in one situation may be used in another situation. The simplest form of transfer occurs when elements of both situations are identical. A more complex form of transfer takes place when elements of two situations are similar. Problem solving in new situations benefits from the degree of congruence that they have to old situations that contain some of the same or similar elements or S-R connections. As the person identifies the congruence between the new and the old, prior connections (previous behaviors) are tried first. Those responses that fit continue to persist in the novel situation. Those that do not fit presumably are not rewarded and are dropped out of the responses to the new stimulus situation.

If one adheres to this approach in teaching, one attempts to include in the curriculum of the school those learning tasks that are common to the widest variety of applications. Subjects that have the greatest amount of transfer potential such as reading or mathematics are emphasized. Obsolete languages or archaic literature and other school subjects that have less transfer potential are of secondary importance; if they are taught at all they emphasize those portions of the subject matter that are transferable. Opportunity for the learner to exercise transfer with appropriate rewards teaches one to transfer.

Permanence Through Effective Use

What determines permanence of learning? The basic answer to the problem of memory is largely based on the empirical findings of memory studies that show decrement in recall over time in the absence of rewarded practice. Thorndike theorized that there was a decay of the S-R connections when they were not used.

The best way to maintain permanence for Thorndike was to periodically practice under rewarding conditions. Accordingly, those connections or bonds that will be most frequently needed in later life should be periodically used and rewarded in order that decay might be minimized.

Spelling words that are learned and then rewarded by daily use are more apt to be remembered than are infrequently used obscure or technical terms. If one wishes to make such words a permanent part of the vocabulary, then one must make sure that the discussions and activities of the day give an opportunity for their regular use.

SKINNER

B. F. Skinner is an exponent of behavioral control for the movement of mankind toward specified goals. He has been termed by many an advocate of cultural engineering. According to Skinner, cultural evolution has proceeded to a large extent by accident. He feels that a scientific society should reject accidental and incidental (as well as tyrannical) manipulation. Skinner believes that we must accept the "fact" that some method of control of human affairs is inevitable. We cannot fully promote the development of man or society unless we have a specified plan.

Skinner has chosen to examine the development of behavior of organisms from an external, operational point of view. Begin with a behavioral act. Examine that behavior and derive its components. Test the adequacy of the derivation by attempting to gradually build the desired behavior in a naive organism. Observe the behavior of the organism after conditioning. Modify the conditioning process as necessary in order to produce the desired behavior. These steps reveal Skinner's disposition toward analysis of complex behavior into the simplest possible overt components. The synthesis of complex behavior is accomplished by the sequential reinforcement of small bits of behavior that approximate the complex act. Skinner believes that the description of virtually all animal behavior, including that of man, is possible by this method. If we can determine the critical simple behaviors that must be reinforced, there is almost no limit — save that of our own patience as behavioral engineers — to what complex behavior patterns can be achieved.

The most effective means of producing the "good"man in the

"good" society is through a systematic application of a reinforcement theory of psychology to the total educational and life experience of man.

Motivation via Reinforcement

Skinner's approach to the problem of motivation is almost completely external to the learner. All complex responses are the result of simple responses being built up into more complicated behavior patterns. Any response that is reinforced is more likely to be repeated whenever the same conditions prevail again. Any set of conditions that promote the reoccurrence of the response is said to be a reinforcement. For example, if a hungry pigeon's behavior is modified by feeding it corn after it makes an appropriate response we can say that corn is a reinforcer. Whatever contingency raises the level of responding or modifies the method of responding is defined as reinforcing.

Two basic types of responses are considered by Skinner: (1) Responses made when a stimulus is known to be eliciting a reflex response (respondent behavior) and (2) responses made when no known preceding stimulus is present (operant behavior). Respondent behavior is dismissed as probably being incidental in the shaping of complex human behavior. With this in mind, the remainder of our discussion of Skinner will deal with operant behavior.

There are natural reinforcers and contrived reinforcers that operate to modify behavior of organisms. Skinner believes that natural reinforcers, while exerting control over behavior, are not necessarily either efficient or moral. In fact, Skinner has stated that the natural reinforcers may be more likely to produce idleness than industry. Furthermore, trivial, useless, exhausting, and harmful behaviors may be learned if natural reinforcers are relied on to shape behavior. Carefully programmed instructional contingencies can and should be arranged to produce desired behavior in organisms.

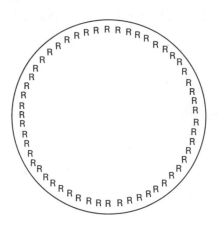

Fig. 3. UNCONDITIONED OPERANTS ARE ASSUMED TO HAVE EQUAL PROBABILITY OF EXPRESSION.

Learning as Reassorting

The basic responses of man consist of small but observable muscle movements. All behavior consists of a complex series of integrated overt movements. For Skinner, in all behavior except respondent (reflex) conditioning these movements are labeled as operants. The untrained organism, as represented in Figure 3, has a vast number of operants (responses) that can be emitted.

Prior to conditioning, these illustrated operants have an essentially equal statistical probability of being made. If any one response is made and reinforced it becomes more likely to be exhibited again under the same conditions than any of the unconditioned operants. This process is diagrammed in Figure 4.

As an example, the complex behavior required in learning to write consists of a number of operants chained together. By selectively reinforcing, the operants making up this complex skill will not only appear more frequently, but the order in which they appear may be built-in or learned (see Figure 5).

Causing an orderly reassortment of operants to occur is the primary task of the Skinnerian educator. He is constantly striving

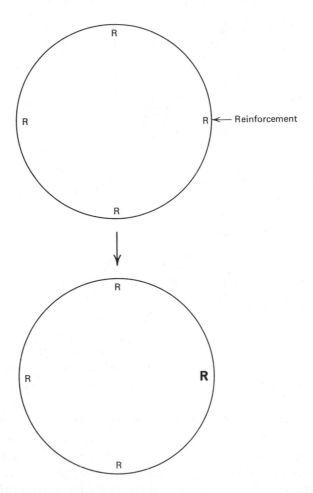

Fig. 4. INCREASING THE RESPONSE RATE OF A SPECIFIC OPERANT THROUGH SELECTIVE REINFORCEMENT.

to build elements of behavior that occur almost at random in the naive learner into patterns prejudged as efficient and effective behavior. These patterns are built up through the reinforcement of sequentially appropriate approximations of the desired behavior. A simple notion of reinforcement is totally inadequate to describe what Skinner means when he considers the operation of

89

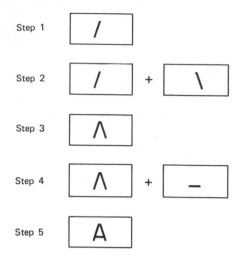

Fig. 5. CHAINING SEQUENCE—LETTER "A".

reinforcement in learning. What kinds of reinforcers are there? What are the most efficient means of arranging contingencies for reinforcement? How much reinforcement is desirable and in what situations?

Skinner has carefully recorded hundreds of thousands of hours of responses of a variety of organisms operating under laboratory conditions. Some of the contingencies (schedules of reinforcement) that Skinner and his associates have studied are continuous, fixed-ratio, variable-ratio, fixed interval, alternative, conjunctive, interlocking, tandem, chained, adjusting, multiple, mixed, interpolated, and concurrent. Each of these patterns of reinforcement shapes behavior in subtly and significantly different ways.

Skinner disavows punishment as an effective means of shaping behavior. He observes that not only education, but the whole of Western culture is moving away from aversive practices. Punishment is probably unnecessary if contingencies of reinforcement are carefully specified and controlled. The major premise of reinforcement theory is that we should arrange conditions under which appropriate behavior is strengthened, but the consequences of punishment do not specify acceptable behavior nor promote its development. To effectively program behavior toward desirable ends, the ends and the means must be carefully specified, tested, and modified.

Facilitation by Programming Reinforcement

According to a Skinnerian approach, the initial phase of an instructional design is to define the terminal behavior. What new or modified behaviors will the learner exhibit after having completed the learning act? Adjusting, recognizing, understanding, having insight when confronted with problems is totally irrelevant and inadequate for Skinner. These cannot be objectives in Skinnerian psychology because such expressions are not overt behaviors. They are not acts that can be measured the way in which Skinner would require a behavior to be measured. Accordingly, a careful and complete description of outcomes in terms of behavioral acts is required before one can begin to promote Skinnerian learning. In other words one must state precisely the overt behaviors sought as outcomes.

After terminal behavior has been specified, a program for causing the behavior to occur can be designed. For Skinner behavior is shaped. One could simply wait for a whole desired behavior to occur and then reinforce it. This would be extremely inefficient. A more effective way of shaping behavior is to reinforce successive approximations of desired behavior. That is, one need not wait for the total desired behavior to be emitted but rather one reinforces intermediate approximations of the final act.

Behavior shaping can be speeded by careful delivery of prompts or clues to the organism and gradually fading out the prompts as the organism learns. After sufficient reinforcement under carefully programmed conditions, prompts can be completely eliminated.

Programming complex behavior requires careful planning and sequencing of material. The sequencing of material in many cases is quite dissimilar to the plans for conventional learning.

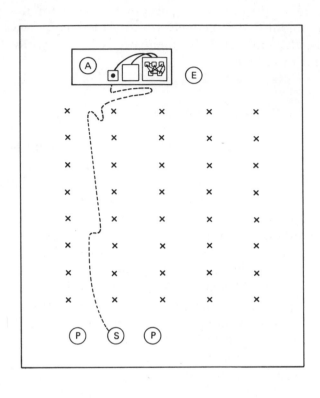

(A) Apparatus

(E) Experimenter

(P) Parent

(S) Child

× Students

——— Route of S

Fig. 6. BEHAVIOR SHAPING DEMONSTRATION.

Psychological sequencing may result in the development of intermediate behaviors that may not be observable in the terminal behavior.

One of the authors devised the following classroom demonstration to illustrate the shaping of behavior by the management of reinforcement. The subject was a two-and-a-half-year-old male whose father was enrolled in a Theories of Learning course. The experimental apparatus consisted of a lever panel connected to a tape recorder. Pressing the lever started ten seconds of contemporary music played by the child's favorite group. The experimenter was able to start and stop the tape recorder by remote control at will. The room set-up is shown in Figure 6.

After the class had assembled and without any preparation of the child the experimenter watched until the child looked towards the front of the room. When he did the music was turned on for a three-second period. After the second playing of the music, the music was withheld until the boy moved forward. As he approached the halfway mark in the room the music started again for three seconds. This time he moved up to the source of the music, which was next to the lever panel. When he looked at the panel the music was again presented. As one would expect he moved to the panel and after a few seconds touched the frame. Again the music played. The second time he touched the frame the music was withheld. An increase in exploratory activity resulted in an incidental touching of the control lever and the music was again turned on by the experimenter. When the music failed to come on again with a gentle touch the boy gave the bar press lever a good stiff hit and the music was activated by the device for ten seconds without the intervention of the experimenter. The initial reinforcement of lever pressing resulted in a sustained approach to the machine for more than 20 minutes without intervention. Interestingly enough the behavior became very selective and the subject would wait patiently for the full music cycle to be completed before hitting the lever again.

The behavior in this demonstration was divided into manageable segments of approaching the front of the room, approaching the control panel, and finally pressing the bar lever. Each step was learned in turn before any new behavior was reinforced and no

93

unrelated behavior was reinforced in this sequence of behavior shaping.

Biological Limits of Reassorting

Skinner places little emphasis on physiologic limits. He acknowledges that physiological limits exist, both interspecies and intraspecies. Skinner's basic concern is utilization of whatever capacities an organism may have. Our present teaching/learning methodologies are highly inefficient. What needs to be done is to design effective programs to develop and utilize the capacities of all men.

Skinner argues that scientists must be permitted to design an environment that will take advantage of man's natural capacity to learn, because he believes they are the only ones who know how to design an environment and condition behavior. In his novel, *Walden Two,* Skinner describes how genetic factors might be favorably structured, but he spends little time on this in comparison to his extensive development of the conditions that control behavior after conception and birth. Ultimately the only significant limit of learning is found in the efficient management of the learning situation, which, stated in simplest terms, is a matter of the right reinforcer in the right place at the right time.

Transfer of Reinforced Operants

The best way to maximize transfer of what is learned to new situations is to build up a very large repertoire of responses in an organism. The reinforcement of a response increases the probability of an organism's making responses containing the same or similar elements. Skinner dislikes the use of terms such as those that claim that a learner has "generalized" or "abstracted" from one situation to another, which imply that we need to "teach" these kinds of "thinking" processes. To simply invoke these terms adds nothing to the science of behavior. They are mentalistic terms that do not explain the processes involved. To Skinner, there is no danger of building up too many responses. A learner must have some behavior to work with. He will be most likely to solve the problems presented by a novel environment if he knows as much as possible about earlier solutions of similar problems. There is no danger that too many facts will overload his mind. Teaching him what others have found need not impair his ability to respond selectively to new situations if a sufficiently powerful teaching technology exists.

We can illustrate one way in which a large repertoire of responses serves a learner by considering the student who, sometime in the past, has been reinforced for doing research in his history class. To the extent that the student was adequately reinforced for learning appropriate research behaviors of using periodical literature guides, microfilm readers, the card catalog, and other tools of the library in searching for documentation for a history research paper he will be able to apply these later. A reinforced operant remains in a person's repertoire unless it is extinguished. When our student is expected to do library research in literature class, he will be able to take advantage of many of the operants that were reinforced by his history class behavior. Behavior will be modified as reinforcers continue to operate or fail to operate in the new situation. New behaviors will, of course, be learned to the extent that they are reinforced as appropriate both to the new situation and to the increased functional behavior of the student.

Permanence Through Intermittent Reinforcement

In accordance with his policy of not engaging in *a priori* theory building, Skinner maintains a distinction between extinction and forgetting. Extinction is the progressive reduction of a reinforced response as a consequence of withholding reinforcement after the emission of that response. This is usually done in a controlled laboratory situation. Extinction generally takes place more quickly than forgetting, which occurs through passive decay. Passive decay differs from extinction in that the organism is not placed in the stimulus situation and is not reinforced for any incidental emissions of a previously reinforced response. The time element in this process is measured more in portions of a lifetime than in weeks, months, or years. Skinner has carried on extensive research on extinction processes following various schedules of reinforcement, and therefore confines most of his work to extinction as a factor in memory as opposed to "true" forgetting.

The extinction process can be dramatically affected by the reinforcement procedure applied. Continuous reinforcement in learning produces relatively strong rates of response in a variety of organisms. Organisms that have been continuously reinforced during training, however, are highly susceptible to rapid extinction of the response. Skinner has found that the variable schedules of reinforcement, particularly variable interval schedules, produce the strongest resistance to extinction. A variable interval schedule is one in which the organism is required to continue responding for differing amounts of time before it is reinforced. A pigeon trained on variable interval reinforcement still exhibited the reinforced behavior several years after the last reinforcement during training. Skinner's writings on teaching and his utopian novel suggest that when a human learning technology equal to what he has achieved in his animal studies is developed, the same kinds of results will be achieved with students.

GESTALT

About the time that Thorndike was deeply involved in his critical studies of learning in America, a number of psychologists in Germany with a strong physiological interest were studying problems in visual perception. One of their major premises was that people respond to whole patterns or situations. Their term for this phenomena, which apparently does not translate literally and directly was "gestalt." These psychologists and their ideas became the Gestalt school of psychology.

Wertheimer, Koffka, and Köhler compiled an impressive array of experimental and empirical information that has resulted in the development of a theory of learning distinct and different from those of the associationists. We shall leave it to the reader to determine whether these differences are differences in levels of description or basic differences about the same set of facts. In either case, the theoretical differences relate to three major considerations.

First, the Gestalt psychologists concerned themselves with the area of perception. They discounted the physical responses of their subjects as the vital elements of experience. Instead, they were concerned with why people responded differentially. As they began to study behavior in terms of why instead of what, they found that individuals looking at the same situation not only responded differently but also reported their experiences differently. On the other hand in the cases where the reported perceptions were highly congruent, the consequent behaviors were similar regardless of the difference in the original situations.

A second major discovery was that more important than either punishment or reward in causing or promoting learning was the degree of ambiguity that the learner perceived. It appears that once one is aware of a degree of ambiguity it becomes very important to reduce the ambiguity. As we shall develop later, it is not the effort, intent, or behavior of the teacher that directly causes learning. Learning is a dynamic process of organizing perceptions to reduce ambiguity (solve problems). Learning is not the mechanical response to external forces that it is for Thorndike and Skinner.

Another point, which comes as a complete reversal of the associationistic psychologies, is the concept that learning starts with a whole and not with a simple part. The whole is more than the sum of the parts; it indicates that one must pay attention to some nonphysical (for example, perceived) dimensions of a situation in addition to the auditory, tactile, visual, olfactory, and gustatory cues.

For example, let us assume that a bicycle consists of a frame, two wheels, pedals, a coaster brake, a chain, handle bars, a sprocket assembly, and one or two fenders. Does adding the parts together produce a bicycle? The answer is in how they are added. If the parts are put (added) into a big box they still do not make a bicycle. One does not have a bicycle in the usual sense until all the parts are assembled or, as the Gestaltists would say, until they are placed in a proper relationship. This proper relationship does not weigh anything. There are no more parts present when they are put together right, but it does make a world of difference especially if one intends to get from here to there on this bicycle.

This rightness of fit is the critical feature of the learning process. As you can imagine, "rightness" is a highly individual thing and is neither absolute nor universal. Insights about relationships may be true, partially true, or false from an external point of view. However, the behaver acts as though they are true until he perceives a necessity to restructure a perceived relationship or "Gestalt." A statement made by one of the authors demonstrates the personal nature of perceptions.

> "As a comfortable middle-aged professor of psychology I have a notion of what proper dress is for me. Since I am comfortable dressing in a conventional way, it is difficult for me to understand why an obvious minority of students I can see from my office window insist on wearing clothing which to me is dirty and ragged and designed to fit a body either much larger or much smaller than the one upon which these unseeming clothes are draped.
>
> On the other hand my own children, who know I get paid a standard salary and know I can afford most of my debts, have trouble understanding my caution about spending every cent over expenses. Being a depression baby (ask your older instructors about this) causes me to perceive the possibility of an economic recession which could impair my ability to provide for my family. The fact there has been no serious economic depression in the past generation doesn't seem to be as important as my perception that it could happen."

Both of these examples indicate how important and individualistic cognitive interpretations are in determining or directing behavior. With these basic concepts in mind, let us look at our basic questions about the learning process and interpret or extrapolate the Gestalt position.

Motivation via Ambiguous Organization

Man is motivated by his inability to satisfactorily relate to a poorly defined situation. Experimental studies have often shown how difficult it is to avoid dealing in some fashion with an incomplete situation. Conduct your own mini-experiment and see how people react to this experience. In twelve years of using this demonstration, groups of college students have always responded in a similar way.

On a chalk board or a piece of paper draw the following figures and label them.

Indicate *A* and say "When I point here, give me the name for this one (point to *B*). Indicate *B* and say, "When I point to this one give me the name for this one (point to *C*). Continue with *D* for *C* and *A* for *D*. Then say, "Let's see how quickly we can go through this twice."

Unless your groups perceive things much differently, when you point to A they will say "circle", to B "square", "trapezoid" for *C,* and "triangle" for *D*.

As you can see by looking at the poorly drawn figures, there are no figures that meet the conventional criteria for a triangle, circle, square, or trapezoid, but these labels fit better than any others and some labels have to be used to meet the demands of the situation. The situation is more complete with these "almost fitting" labels and therefore subjects can continue with other aspects of the problem.

Instead of being repelled by imperfect and incomplete things and ideas, we seem to be attracted to such situations, objects, and people. The unknown and, therefore, incompletely understood stands as a beacon on the ocean of man's experience luring him to death and destruction or to glory and knowledge with equal frequency.

At this writing the press is on in higher education for undergraduates to experience drugs for mind expansion and student power for increased political and social involvement. If these are not the burning issues when you read this book, you should have little trouble in finding the unknown but perhaps knowable grail of your day.

The prime motivator then is the desire to organize the universe as one perceives it. When one believes it to be effectively organized, he will not search for change nor will he organize anew or learn any more than he knew before.

The teacher's task becomes one of helping students to assess the effectiveness of their perceptual organizations of the universe. If this is done in a supportive environment the children are likely to respond with vigorous and vital inquiry—the soul of "discovery."

Learning as Perceptual Organization

As we have suggested, learning for the Gestaltist is a matter of organizing perceptual patterns. This desire to organize perceptions seems to be universal and biological in nature. If a person has his universe well ordered with no loose ends or troubling experiences left unresolved, it can be assumed he has learned all that he is aware he needs to know at that moment. He is not, and need not be, involved in a learning (organizing) experience.

Suppose some one comes along and does something that a person perceives as upsetting to his universe. If the notion of closure applies, we can expect him to do something to restore a measure of order to his psychologically perceived environment. Learning is a process of moving from an inadequate organization to a more adequate organization.

In the changing responsibilities of the student in American education, we can trace this process of organization, evaluation, reorganization, and reevaluation. Let us examine a traditional pattern of educational experience. Typically, the primary responsibility of the elementary school pupil is to do what he is told to do. If he accepts this organization he seldom has problems with the conventional teacher. The instructions or demands are usually made on a day-by-day basis with an almost constant checking by the teacher.

What happens when the youngster carries this organization to the high school? If he waits to be told each day what he should do for the following day, or if he waits for the teacher to do a daily check on the progress he is making on some long term project he is likely to be less then successful in his high school experience.

The transition to college or university scholarship is one that again calls for a rather abrupt reorganization mandated by a set of changing conditions. The college student who must rely on the academic judgment of his professor or the professor's approval for every academic adventure is less likely to capture the essential experience of being educated at the university level.

The shifting responsibility or the learning of new academic roles is essentially a dynamic process of reorganizing patterns of behavior that have become inadequate. Although this example has been cast in a frame of reference incompatible with Gestalt psychology, the behavior cited does reflect the process of change from inadequate to more adequate organization.

The technical label for the principle described, which is basic to Gestalt theory, is the *Law of Pragnanz*. This law suggests that persons tend to organize their perceptions to form more complete or perceptually adequate gestalts (patterns, configurations, or organizations of perceptions). A good or perceptually adequate gestalt has regularity, simplicity, stability. There are subsidiary principles of organization that should be taken into account when systematically applying Gestalt theory to a learning situation. They are similarity, proximity, closure, and good continuation. Each of these subsidiary principles plays a part in the formation of "good" gestalts in the cognitive field of the behaver. Learning is a restructuring of the field. This process of restructuring is a cognitive process in which insights or "hypotheses" are acted on by the behaver. If a hypothesis is supported, then it is accepted as "true" for the person until it no longer results in reduced ambiguity in problem solving.

Facilitation Through Reduction of Ambiguity

Essentially there are four operations that one person can perform that may help another to learn.

Present a problematic situation. If a teacher presents a situation which the learner accepts as vital and relevant, then by definition the student is motivated and has no recourse but to attempt to include this problem in his perceptual field. The easiest thing for him to do is to cope with the situation by using extant patterns of perception. If this should fail, then he will need to find a new way of behaving.

Define a specific problem. In either of the above cases the teacher should assume his second responsibility, that of assisting the student in defining a specific manageable problem, preferably stated in behavioral terms. Should the child be permitted to define an unsolvable problem, learning could not take place. If the problem were defined in only a general and vague way, it might take a lifetime to solve it. If a specific problem were defined in ambiguous terms, the student would have little success in identifying effective study or resolution of the problem.

Evaluate procedures. With a specific problem in mind and the ends-means stated in relevant terms, the mentor can facilitate effective learning by participating in teacher–student evaluations of the procedures. Many blind alleys can be avoided and countless hours of unfruitful investigation may be eliminated if at the right point the educator asks simply and directly, "How are you going to approach this problem?" and "Why are you going to do it this way?" Both of these questions keep the attention of the learner focused on the specific issue at hand and protect him from the accumulation of an overwhelming array of nongoal-directed questions and answers.

Evaluate outcomes. The final step in promoting effective behavior is to involve the learner in an assessment focused on how well he has solved the problem he set out to solve. Without this step much learning is minimized. Have you ever walked away from a problem when it was resolved to someone else's satisfaction but not to your own? The usual response is to deny the whole experience as a relevant one. This might account for students of all ages who respond to the question, "What did you get from school today?" with such answers as, "An 87 in a biology test," "A," or "C" in psychology," or perhaps, "I failed the midterm." If more teachers were aware of how helpful concurrent assessment can be they might feel less like tormentors and more like mentors.

The essence of experience lies in perception. The significance of perceptions rests in their amenability to the development of relational analyses. Learning, when it is meaningful, is not an isolated experience in the present, but a present experience related to our previous conditions as well as those we anticipate.

The identification of principles derived through the solution of a problem is the distillation of the essence of many individual experiences having some degree of perceptual identity.

When learning is geared towards: "doing this thing so I will learn more about all problems of this type," a general kind of learning is experienced. On the other hand when the learner views the situation as "I just want to solve this problem as quickly as I can," it results in very specific and less useful learning.

In summary, others can help the learning process by enlarging the number and kind of problems the learner perceives. They can help by promoting specific behavioral goals, relevant procedures, and effective means of evaluating outcomes. All of these functions facilitate the learner's organization of new perceptions without in any way imposing the particular perceptions of the teacher. In effect, the teacher challenges the student to show how he intends to learn with as much dispatch and facility as can be mustered.

Biological Limits of Cognitive Organization

What one can learn in a lifetime is a function of the condition of one's physical equipment. If one is blind then there will be many visual organizations that will be modified or limited in the overall learning experience. If there is a central nervous system impairment that impinges on any perceptual input or output operation, then again the extent of learning is altered or diminished.

For the vast majority of healthy unimpaired individuals the ultimate limits of learning are related to such complex sensory and perceptual systems that it is rare for anyone to reach the point in his lifetime when it is impossible to organize and incorporate new information into his perceptual field.

In spite of this optimistic interpretation of the limits of learning, we all have experienced those days when we felt we could not or did not learn. Apparently there are temporary physical or emotional states that interfere with learning. Of greater educational significance are the negative effects of long-term expectation of marginal success or failure. The learner will be limited in his learning and learning opportunities to the extent that he does not expect to adequately cope with life as he finds it.

Learning is impaired for the healthy well-adjusted person if he is permitted to approach an ambiguous situation without a plan of attack or evaluation. Ambiguity in doses that can be dealt with is the challenge of life. Ambiguity in amounts or kinds that lead to further indecision is the essence of pessimism and defeatism, both of which fail to serve as motivators of personally satisfying socially relevant behavior.

Transfer as Transposition

The usefulness of what is learned is a function of the principles or generalizations generated by learning experiences. No situation is ever repeated from a Gestalt point of view. In such routine things as driving to work you are in a very real perceptual sense not doing it "again." You may be driving and this driving may involve many familiar relationships, but the fact that yesterday you got a ticket for running that red light or that you did not get caught running it alters this day's experience and makes it a nonrepetitive act.

What you have derived from many driving experiences over

many occasions is an awareness of the many factors related to your driving behavior. Traffic comes at you slowly and rapidly, you have faced little cars and large trucks. All of these experiences blend together into your personal notion of what it means to drive. Therefore, when you meet a military convoy that includes some lumbering tanks with those terrifying cannons leveled at your car, your previous perceptions enable you to cope with the situation as long as they keep to the right and do not discharge their weapons. All you have learned before is useful as long as whatever you face acts in accord with vehicular traffic law and custom.

Let us consider an example in which the original learning involves the evaluation of the specific experiences but not a search for the basic principles common to the experiences. Suppose a flying school teaches you how to fly a specific plane and gives you many hours of experience in taking off and landing this craft on a private air strip. If this instruction is specific and if no principles are explained or drawn out, how likely would you be to successfully take off and land in a commercial airport with heavy traffic?

Some of you may have a great deal of faith in incidental learning, so let us further dramatize the situation by assuming that the plane you learned to fly was a World War I open cockpit no radio biplane and a private twin jet will be used to test you. As ridiculous as this example seems, many teachers teach subjects with methods designed solely for the purpose of passing academic tests and believe themselves to be successfully preparing young people to live effective lives. The most limiting factor in restricting the usefulness of learning is to teach it with the intent not to generalize it or relate it to other subject matter and life experiences.

That some teachers are teaching this way is beyond question because often teachers have said they were bored with what they were teaching since they had taught it before. Apparently their purpose in learning the subject matter was to learn it well enough to get someone else to pass a test on the material. Naturally, all subsequent experiences can bring no further closure and teachers and students are honor bound to reorganize and honor the useless mass of repetitive acts of nonlearning.

Permanence as a Function of Perceptual Stability

What is learned is never forgotten. Much of what is learned is altered and modified by things that happen after the initial learning. The question of permanence has to be restated: What determines the relevance and availability of any learned pattern?

The answer is found in the manner in which it is learned. Items learned in isolation, without regard for significance or relationship to other ideas or experiences become not forgotten but so obscured that they are rarely if ever available to the learner.

Learning done within the problem-solving and principle-development paradigm has built into it "mental hooks" that permit us to bring it back into a central perceptual position in order to examine it for relevance to the problems (ambiguities) of the day.

Material that can be redintegrated days, weeks, months, and years afterwards is usually the most relevant and, therefore, is probably what most people could describe as more permanent.

Apparently, we remember everything we have learned that has relevance for our present condition. If we learn it and need it, we remember it. Songs learned as a novice camper around a first campfire are remembered and used as long as the joy and enthusiasm of the experience persist as a perceptual pattern for the camper. If he grows too old to camp or if he becomes a non-camper, those once vital songs are no longer relevant, they are no longer central to him, and he does not sing them or "remember" them.

That they may be filed away instead of lost is evidenced by the flood of "remembered" songs that come back to all of us who have once enjoyed camping and the fellowship of singing when we find ourselves confronted by accident or design with a campfire, companions, and songs that need to be sung.

The implication for making classroom learning permanent seems to be that teachers and parents should generate the kind of intellectual and emotional environment for children that requires them to perceive themselves as people who have learned and must use their learning in everyday living.

Teachers and parents who plan experiences that come to an

end can expect a tremendous "loss" of related learning. The teacher in preparing children to pass a test sets the limit on how long the material should and will be remembered. The parent who teaches the child to be good in church is inviting a change of perceptual pattern as soon as they get home with a very quick loss of goodness.

COMBS AND SNYGG

Another more contemporary field theory is that formulated by Snygg and Combs in 1949. The phenomenological[1] approach to educational practice has become, in the past twenty years, a source of new direction as educators continue to seek greater understanding of the teaching–learning process. Although both phenomenological and Gestalt psychology fit into the field theory pattern, Combs and Snygg, by placing emphasis on personalistic factors, have produced a distinctly different approach to learning and behavior.

Phenomenologists see man as an organism forever seeking greater personal adequacy. The search for adequacy or self-actualization is the driving force motivating all of man's behavior. This search for a sense of adequacy is not a selfish process in which the expansion of self takes place at the expense of others.

Although a man may have felt adequate yesterday, he sees himself as a purposive being who needs to change to be ready to meet the unexpected challenges of today. So merely statically maintaining an unchanging self is not enough. Man must strive to enhance his perceived self so that he feels that he can behave effectively in terms of his own goals and purposes. Man, in the process of becoming more adequate, becomes enriched as a self through increased transaction with aspects of his perceptual environment including other people previously perceived as not self-related. The adequate personality is one that embodies positive percepts of self, a clearly developing concept of self, a growing acceptance of self and identification with others, and finally a rich, varied, and available perceptive field of experience.

[1] Other terms representing substantially the same approach to behavior are perceptual psychology, humanistic psychology, third-force psychology.

LEARNING AS SELF-ENHANCEMENT.

Motivation via Inadequate Differentiation

Phenomenologically speaking (that is, from the behaver's view) one is never unmotivated. Every person is continually seeking personal adequacy. However, to a teacher a child may appear to "lack motivation." Anyone at that point who was not doing what the teacher thought was of primary importance in promoting the teacher's concept of the adequate student would appear "unmotivated." Combs and Snygg note that from an external point of view it may seem doubtful or even absurd that people are always seeking a personal sense of adequacy—attempting to enhance themselves. A delinquent youngster may appear to others to be seeking self-destruction. For the child, however, the swaggering hostile acting out behavior is a way of coping with a threatening situation. In a sense, such an "inadequate" person "whistling in the dark" is doing the best he knows how to do under the conditions in which he finds himself and in any case is highly motivated and active in the process of seeking adequacy.

In most cases, the teacher is not confronted with highly inadequate children who define adequacy the way he does. To many children, learning their French or spelling has little personal reference to them. When faced with the punishments of failure, they may perform just well enough to escape the threat. A change in perception occurs, to be sure, but hardly an ideal learning situation!

Learning as Perceptual Differentiation

Learning is a change in the phenomenal field or psychological world of the behaver. Perceptually speaking, these changes are brought about by progressive differentiation. By differentiation, we refer to the process of bringing a particular perception into clearer figure in the phenomenal field. This process occurs at all levels of complexity from the controlled laboratory experiments involving the manipulation of few variables to the problem-solving behavior of man in a multivariate situation.

Learning, as a process of differentiation, moves from the gross to the refined. Consider, for example, several possible perceptions of the word "child," which some person might consider to be most self-related at different times in his life. Observe the continued process of differentiating in new contexts in each instance. At point one of the concept "what I am" may be quite adequate. At a second phase the previously differentiated percepts of "child" are no longer sufficient, because one does not think of himself as a child. The original perception is not gone: it is just no longer the most functional or adequate one. By the time we get to illustration number six this person finds his perception of his

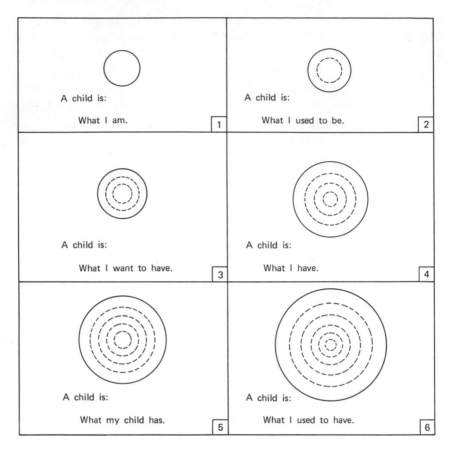

Fig. 7. CONTINUITY OF DIFFERENTIATION.

grandchild to be his most functional definition of the word "child." All of the previous definitions exist and can be used to communicate with others, but the most personal meaning of the word relates to his current role.

Changing of perceptions or learning is a function of need of the behaver. Merely presenting material to another is not sufficient to cause him to learn. External rewards and other factors outside the learner may temporarily modify behavior. External manipulation of the environment does not from the behaver's view "cause" his response. In the learner's eyes, his acts are defined as the best way to satisfy his immediate need. Underlying all conscious and immediate needs is the maintenance and enhancement of self. It it important to realize that although a learner may appear to the teacher to be learning to improve his performance on a school lesson, he may really be maintaining his self-concept by appearing to be interested and thus keeping out of "trouble." The analysis of learning must always involve an appraisal from the student's point of view.

Facilitation Through Self-Enhancement

Teaching is the facilitation of perceptual differentiation or a change in meaning. Teaching is not a direct act. One cannot hand a perception to another person or cause one to occur. For the teacher in a perceptual context, the problem of teaching is not, "How do I present the subject matter?" so much as it is, "How can I help students perccive personal meaning of the subject matter (scc it as related in some way to their lives)?"

It must be remembered that what is learned is a function of need. Need, in turn, is what is perceived as maintaining and enhancing to the self. Accordingly, those learnings that are not perceived as self-related are of only peripheral significance for the learner if indeed they are of significance at all.

There are many factors that do facilitate the exploration of personal meaning in a learning situation. Some of these are freedom from threat, an atmosphere of acceptance, the security of limits, acceptance of mistakes as part of the learning process, and an appreciation of the uniqueness of the individual and his potential for developing personally relevant perceptions new to him.

Perceptual psychologists are committed to the postulate that there is no one way of creating effective relationships with students (that is, no one correct specific way of behaving). This is a recognition of the uniqueness of the teacher and the learner. To deny this uniqueness would be to negate a basic precept of phenomenological psychology. An effective way of behaving for one teacher cannot be assumed to be effective for another.

Lest this seem like an affirmation of the notion that teachers are born not made, let us hasten to say that such a view is highly inconsistent with phenomenological psychology. Rather, the phenomenologist would suggest that we can improve the quality of instruction by helping teachers better understand feelings and perceptions, their own and those of their students. By this process we can facilitate the exploration and transactional discovery of personal meaning for the teacher and students and thus create learning environments that are relevant for both.

Biological Limits of the Phenomenal Field

In a classic paper on intelligence, Combs noted that intelligence could be profitably viewed as a functional dynamic of perception. There are dynamic and static factors that do limit one's ability to perceive. The physiological factors that define an upper limit for intelligence, except for the case of the brain damaged or the genetic defective, impose no observable limits on man's ability to make differentiations. On the other hand, there are certain practical factors that may, in a sense, limit the differentiation of the perceptive field of the behaver. Among these are time, need, opportunity, goal and values, self-perceptions, and threat.

According to the phenomenological point of view, differentiation within the field requires time enough for a personal experience with an event. Please note that this confrontation with an experience is conceived of in terms of the behaver's point of view. A child may appear to be confronting the problems of studying multiplication outside the temporal limits the teacher sees as being reasonable and proper. He is also busy perceiving and incorporating a variety of percepts in addition to the arithmetic facts involved, which may demand temporal dimensions for the experience the teacher cannot anticipate.

The ultimate need of an individual is to maintain and enhance the phenomenal self. The person throughout his life is continually striving for further actualization of self. Therefore, any attempt to list finite and particular specific needs is futile for phenomenal field psychologists, since this list would ultimately

112

become as long as the total number of *person-situation encounters* in which a behaver will be involved during his lifetime. Since all that the person does is seen by him as maintaining the self, those factors that become more self-related are more readily learned and retained than those that are less self-related. The person learns best that which he perceives a need to know, that is, that which maintains the self.

Environment and opportunity influence perceptions. There are at least two types of environmental effect—the actual events and the symbolic or vicarious event.

Actual experiences are those in which the learner has the opportunity to directly experience the sensory and perceptual dimensions (qualities) of an immediate situation. Vicarious or symbolic experience is one in which the learner has the opportunity to experience the perceptual dimensions of a situation on an immediate basis and to experience the sensory dimensions on an interpretive plane.

In the actual experience the problem might be defined, "It's too hot in here! What can I do about it?" The vicarious experience would give rise to a statement of the problem in the following terms: "If it were too hot in here, what could I do about it?" Either or neither of these "problems" can be "real" for the learner or meaningless, depending on how he relates to the experience.

If a vicarious experience has greater personal meaning for a person, it can have a more dynamic impact on his perceptions and behavior than direct experiences that are perceived as having less personal meaning.

The goals and values of an individual affect his perceptions. Goals come from experiences—that is from the person's interpretations of his experiences—not the experiences per se. The culture in which one grows, of course, deeply affects the goals a person holds, because it is one of the variables that confirms or denies the learner's expectations and desires. But the person does not behave purely in terms of the verbalized goals and values of the social order in which he lives. He develops goals and values that he has differentiated through experience as satisfying his perceived needs. These goals may be simple or complex, they may be implicit or explicit, they may be positive or negative.

Individual goals are always unique to the personality of the behaver. The more stable the culture and the clearer the social goals then the more stable and consistent the goals and values of individuals. In a modern society undergoing rapid growth or change, there are more opportunities for conflicts and disruptions of goals and values. However, in order to achieve some stability the effective personality tends to develop goals and values which, although open to change, provide him with a measure of stability for judging his action and that of others.

What the person perceives as the reality of his self-concept contributes to or detracts from his utilization of his potentialities. Counselors, teachers, and others who work with children are aware of the powerful effects that an individual's estimate of his worth and abilities has on his personal and social functioning. A child who has come to see himself as a "nonreader" will behave as though this label represents immutable fact. A person who sees himself as a poor speaker will have great difficulty changing this perception once it has been well formed and personally confirmed in spite of objective assurances from others. Indeed percepts of self once crystallized are slow to change. Successful experiences that have personal meaning to the behaver are crucial in the development of an expanding, growing personality. The experiences that help the individual to perceive himself as capable of dealing with problems prepare him to face the future with confidence. Experiences that cause the person to feel inadequate generate the expectation of threat.

Threat is defined as a set of interpretations that cause a person to restrict his perceptual field and to exhibit defensive behavior. To the extent that these two factors lead to rigidity of behavior and inability to consider new methods of attacking problems, they severely limit the learner's potential in a particular situation.

It is important to note a crucial difference between threat and challenge. A threatened person feels that his self is in jeopardy, and he feels essentially helpless to deal constructively with the perceived threat. The same "objective" situation may be faced by another person (who has a more adequate perception of self, and a richer, more varied, more available field of experiences) as an exciting problem to be solved. The second person may be threatened little, if at all, since he expects to cope with the situation.

A challenge is a set of interpretations in which the learner perceives a need to do something differently than he is doing. He must also feel that he *can* do something to bring about a personally satisfying resolution of the problem he sees.

Again, an outside observer may see the situation as essentially the same for both persons, but in terms of the way it is differentially experienced by the two people it is dramatically discrete.

Transfer as Relevance

The value of an educational experience is determined by the self-relatedness of the learning. Subject matter that is seen as being external or apart from the person will have little transferability to new learning situations where it may be used in the resolution of novel problems. Subject matter learned only to avoid failure or punishment results in behavior so situationally specific that it has little value beyond the moment. The percepts that the person holds concerning himself also affect the usefulness of what is learned. As indicated in the earlier discussion of threat and challenge, the adequate person sees himself as essentially able to cope with life. For a person with negative self-attitudes a specific situation might be perceived as threatening and overpowering; whereas the same circumstances might be seen as a thrilling challenge for an adequate person. The person who is open to his world and who has a variety of positive, self-related learnings is better able to attack and solve new problems. Therefore, the task of the teacher is not so much to assure that content is covered but rather to foster situations in which students will be able to have personally meaningful socially significant experiences with the content.

Much of the content of formal education is fundamentally irrelevant to the basic self-concept of the students involved. The conflict between the expressed mores of the culture and the expectations of the school makes much of school learning relevant for classroom roles but not for out-of-class social or civic roles.

115

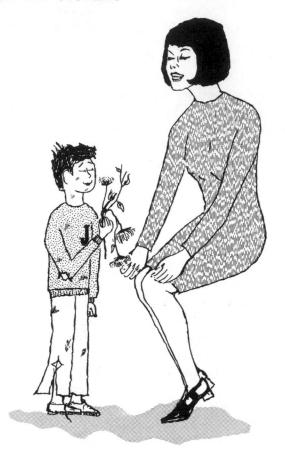

PERSONAL DIFFERENTIATION. IF HE IS YOUR SON IT WILL ALWAYS BE THE MOST BEAUTIFUL BOUQUET IN THE WORLD.

Except for the rare person, not many young ladies perceive electronics or chemistry as a major contribution to their life roles of seductive sirens or liberated females. Assuredly some inroads are being made by requiring these courses for college entrance. How many colleges can brag about the number of women nonmajors selecting either of these areas as an unrestricted elective? It also appears that it may be some time yet before the average housewife will hurry to the fuse box in the basement and begin a systematic search for the blown fuse when the electricity goes off in the middle of the afternoon.

With just about the same regularity, the young adult male is found who will proudly present his efforts at poetry to his peers for their edification. Few will even admit they enjoy reading poetry assignments. Excellence in literature courses is a predominantly feminine domain according to outward appearances. It just is not sex-role relevant for the robust swinger or stalwart family provider to spend much time creating or reading poetry except as a specialized premarital or academic experience.

A critical review of the discrepancy between social-cultural expectations and classroom activities might account for a large portion of the assumption many teenagers make—learning is something done for school and what is learned there is next to useless in "real" life.

Permanence as Continuity

Differentiations once made are permanent. One cannot "unperceive." There is no postulation of a "decay" principle in phenomenological psychology. As a general rule, simple perceptions are made more complex through a process of differentiation in which gross perceptions are made more detailed. This occurs because the preceding simpler perceptions become inadequate and, therefore, less meaningful than complex ones. Simple concepts may be less available in the field than later, more complex, more meaningful perceptual patterns. They may be less available, but they are not in any sense destroyed. Ideas remembered are those available; ideas forgotten are those unavailable for use in solving present problems.

When one remembers, the event is not remembered. Instead an experiencing of the event is remembered. Memory is subjective because of the percepts held at the time of the event, and also because of the highly personal effects of intervening experiences on the present perceptual organization.

The best way to insure that a perception once differentiated will be available in the future is to arrange the circumstances for learning so that the learner perceives a need for achieving a variety of meaningful personal experiences. Again, we cannot hand learners experiences that are meaningful, but we can attempt to engender situations so that there is opportunity for such learning to occur.

We observed a clinical demonstration in hypnosis that effectively illustrates how experiences that appear to have been forgotten may be recalled. The subject in the demonstration was experiencing regression to a period in early childhood that reportedly could not be recalled. The clinician was able to facilitate the revivication of the experience by helping the client to reinstate a regressive series of self-perceptions that were remembered and verbalized. The client was able ultimately to reexperience the occurrence and to adopt the perceptions he had as a child during that period. It is noteworthy that the client did not speak as a child, however, but retained his adult speech patterns. Such an example shows how, given the need to recall and appropriate ways of facilitating recall, the person was able to remember previously unavailable material. This case serves to reveal how recall of past experience takes into account intervening experiences. One cannot go back to a former state in a complete sense, because the self-image has grown and changed and must inevitably influence the recall of any prior experience. But previous experiences are not lost and gone forever.

PRIMARY SOURCES FOR FURTHER READING

Associationist Systems

Holland, James J., and Skinner, B. F. *The Analysis of Behavior.* New York: McGraw-Hill, 1961.

Skinner, B. F. *The Behavior of Organisms.* New York: Appleton-Century, 1938.

Skinner, B. F. *Cumulative Record.* New York: Appleton-Century-Crofts, 1959.

Skinner, B. F. *Science and Human Behavior.* New York: Macmillan, 1953.

Skinner, B. F. *The Technology of Teaching*. New York: Appleton-Century-Crofts, 1968.

Thorndike, Edward L. *Animal Intelligence*. New York: Macmillan, 1911.

Thorndike, Edward L. *Educational Psychology*. Vol. II. New York: Teachers College, Columbia University, 1913.

Thorndike, Edward L. *Selected Writings from a Connectionist's Psychology*. New York: Appleton-Century-Crofts, 1949.

Field Systems

Combs, Arthur W., Ed. *Perceiving, Behaving, Becoming*. Association for Supervision and Curriculum Development: The Association, 1962.

Combs, Arthur W. *The Professional Education of Teachers*. Allyn and Bacon, 1965.

Combs, Arthur W., and Snygg, Donald. *Individual Behavior*. rev. ed. New York: Harper, 1959.

Koffka, Kurt. *Principles of Gestalt Psychology*. New York: Harcourt, Brace, 1935.

Köhler, Wolfgang. *Gestalt Psychology*. New York: Liveright, 1947.

Lewin, Kurt. *Field Theory in Social Science; Selected Theoretical Papers*. D. Cartwright. ed. New York: Harper, 1951.

Wertheimer, Max. *Productive Thinking*. New York: Harper, 1959.

BRIEFER INTRODUCTIONS TO THEORETICAL FORMULATIONS

Associationist Systems

Skinner, B. F. "Freedom and the Control of Men." *American Scholar,* **25,** pp. 47–65.

Skinner, B. F. "Why We Need Teaching Machines." *Harvard Educational Review,* **31,** pp. 377–398.

Thorndike, Edward L. "Mental Discipline in High School Studies." *Journal of Educational Psychology,* **15,** 1–22, 83–88.

Thorndike, Edward L. "Reward and Punishment in Animal Learning." *Comparative Psychology Monographs,* **8,** No. 39.

Field Systems

Combs, Arthur W. "Intelligence from a Perceptual Point of View." *Journal of Abnormal and Social Psychology,* **47,** pp. 662–673.

Kohler, Wolfgang. "Gestalt Psychology Today." *American Psychologist,* **14,** pp. 727–734.

Lewin, Kurt. "Field Theory and Learning." *The Psychology of Learning.* National Society for the Study of Education. Forty-first Yearbook. Part II, 1942, pp. 215–242.

Rogers, Carl R. "The Place of the Person in the New World of the Behavioral Sciences." *Personnel and Guidance Journal,* **39,** pp. 442–451.

Snygg, Donald. "The Need for a Phenomenological System of Psychology." *Psychological Review,* **48,** pp. 404–424.

SET FOUR

Congruent Philosophies and Theories

PROLOGUE: THE VALUE OF COMPATIBLE THEORY AND PHILOSOPHY

The basic elementary concepts outlined in the previous set implicitly indicate the internal consistency of each theory. Any theory comprised of parts that do not fit together or of incompatible dynamic relationships is as ineffective as a vehicle made from bicycle parts powered by a jet engine. It might look all right as long as it was not expected to do anything.

The description of the three basic philosophies in Set Two also demonstrates how different but internally consistent concepts

---

[1] Although we have chosen to use the term learning theory very broadly, it is only fair and accurate to indicate that Skinner, and Combs and Snygg agree that behavior is a more appropriate designation than learning. For them learning theory denotes a narrow interpretation of the processes of change in the human organism more relevant for the earlier experimental work of the Thorndikian and Gestalt systems. Since the term behavior has been associated with behavior therapy and behavior theory, we refer to all the systems presented as learning theories. We offer our apologies (in the original Greek sense of the word) to all who would prefer other labels.

121

about the nature of man, society, and education can be formulated. Each of these philosophies serves as a reasonable orientation for educational practice only to the extent that the assumptions about the nature of society (man in the collective) is an extension of the notion of man. Interpretations of education must be compatible with and related to both man and society.

Educational practice as we have experienced it is generated as an artistic approximation of the goals of education defined by educational philosophy through the use of relevant and appropriate means delineated by a compatible learning theory.

This assumption imposes two sets of restrictions on the teaching behavior of the professional educator.

What he does must be designed to accomplish the purposes of education to which he is committed. He is not free to use behaviors that negate the ends of education. He is free to experiment with new approaches to determine the extent to which the ends selected are promoted.

What he does must not violate what he assumes to be the learning processes of the learner. His teaching behaviors must not include elements that are impossible for the student to utilize in his learning. Experimentation to determine the relevance and effectiveness of a given teaching behavior for the learner is a valid method of extending knowledge, but the learner's investment in the learning experience must be protected from unreasonable and unwarranted risks.

By evidencing an uncanny skill in compartmentalizing conflicting ends and means a few teachers create a catalog of syncratic learning experiences. Some of these serve the educational goals of the teacher. Other experiences, although compatible with the learning theory of the teacher, are incompatible with his goals. It seems to be an obvious statement to make, but the means that one uses should be dynamically related to the ends or values chosen. If philosophy and theory (ends and means statements) are incompatible, then any technique predicated on these two conflicting facets is very likely to produce undesirable or unexpected results. These results are usually expressed in terms of ineffective or incidental learning behavior.

Suppose a teacher selects a trip to an observatory as a learning experience. Assume his end is an apprecation of the work of the great astronomers. Conjecture further that the child, once in the observatory, is given complete license to roam around the building being told only that his final grade in science depends on his performance on an objective test to be given later.

Is there anything invalid about having an awareness and appreciation of the work of the great astronomers as a part of the general education of the public school student? Is there anything inappropriate with testing him to see how well the teacher has engineered the learning situation? Both this goal and this technique are relevant to at least one philosophy and one theory and seem to be compatible with each other. When we look at the intervening behavior on the part of the teacher and the student, it is difficult to see how wandering about on one's own could but incidentally be related to the prescribed examination. On the other hand, it is difficult to define an exploratory visit to an observatory as a worthless experience. With some other goal in mind such an experience could promote worthwhile learning.

In any case, we shall assume that our learner does poorly on the examination. How would one go about assessing the work element in this learning experience? Should we discard the purpose? Should we change the examination? Should we simply fail the youngster? Perhaps the intervening experience needs to be modified, but:

> If all the elements in the formulation remain flexible and if the elements may exist independently with equal validity then there is no way to improve the experience because improvement itself cannot be defined without some reference point.
>
> If, on the other hand, some dimension of the sequence has priority (usually the philosophical or end function), then one can begin a rational evaluative procedure. If the end is "good" and it has not been achieved, then it is more profitable to investigate the means used.

If the ends and means used are both valid and compatible, then failure in education may reasonably be attributed to sociopathic or psychopathic dimensions of the learner's personality. In such cases educational remediation must involve noninstructional support staff and techniques before effective instruction is likely to result in effective learning. Nothing is more futile than trying to change school practices (either theory or philosophy) in order to establish effective instructional programs for children needing therapeutic intervention.

Inherent in these statements is a possibility of gross misinterpretation. Philosophy and theory are more directive than restrictive. To have ends and means compatible does not mean that educational practice is predetermined and fixed. If a philosophy states that a student must accept responsibility, and learning theory suggests that this is best done through a series of graduated experiences, the teacher has not been restricted to any unreasonable degree. He must work toward the end of having each student accept responsibility. He must also facilitate each child's experience through a series of increasingly more responsible activities. He is free to decide the how, when, where, and what of the experiences. Only the general end and the general method are specified. The several thousand degrees of freedom left for the average teacher to exercise in a typical day of instruction offer the most creative of teachers a very open field in which to develop artistic interpretations and implementations of the mandate imposed by the consistency of theory and practice.

Effective education practice has as its basic hallmarks three fundamental characteristics.

1. It moves the learner towards the defined goals of the educational experience.
2. It uses methods that enable the child to learn effectively.
3. It accepts a variety of techniques within the limits of the philosophy and theory involved.

In the section to follow various relationships among the theories and philosophies will be introduced with the intention of

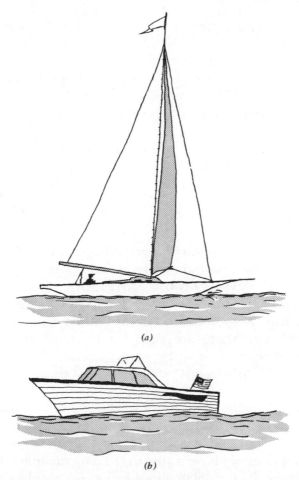

(a)

(b)

AN INTERPRETATION OF MOTIVATION: A CHOICE OF MODELS. (A) USE OF EXTERNAL FORCES; (B) USE OF IN-TERNAL FORCES.

helping the reader to reassess or develop the theoretical and philosophical bases of his professional educational practices.

MOTIVATION: EXTERNAL VERSUS INTERNAL

The labels external and internal are applied to the two general psychological conceptions of the source of motivation for

125

organisms. By these terms we mean either that the person is conceived of as being motivated by factors outside or within himself. A comparison of associationisms and field systems shows that, in general, associationists accept external sources of motivation as more crucial. The field systems, on the other hand, strongly favor an internal approach to motivation.

EXTERNAL

Thorndike

Man is viewed as a reactive organism motivated by rewards delivered from the external environment. These rewards act as forces that come to mold his behavior. Learning is a mechanistic act. Stimuli and responses become connected through the operation of rewards. Responses not rewarded are exhibited less frequently. Although there are deprivation states that impel the organism into reaction, it is the external environment that provides the stimuli to which a person or an animal responds in a learning situation.

The traditionalist philosophies hold that man should live in accord with absolute truth. There is some basis for agreement then that man responds to something larger than and outside himself. Man does not have a role in shaping the universe according to idealism. Rather, man should discover absolute truth and live in tune with it. In terms of motivation, these philosophers and Thorndike agree that motivation is determined by forces other than those that the learner brings to the situation.

The technological philosophy's mechanical conception of the universe and of behaving organisms is very compatible with a Thorndikian view of man as a reactive organism capable of complex mechanical reasoning. For the realist, natural law exists. In order for man to survive and prosper he should uncover as much of natural law as possible. He then can live a natural life in harmony with the laws of the universe, which are fixed. Man does not shape the cosmos; he discovers and uses what is there. Since

126

Thorndike's theory of learning views man as essentially a reactive receiver of the environment, his views on motivation are held in common with the realists.

Since man is viewed as a reactive organism there is a fundamental difference between Thorndike and the transactional philosophies. The view of the person as passively reacting to rewarding stimuli that impinge on him is far from the transactional view that man interprets, interacts, modifies, and extrapolates his environment. This view of man as a blank organism responding to environmental pressures without personalistic transpositions is in conflict with the transactional interpretation that motivation is primarily an internal matter. The basic conflict between connectionism and transactionalism results in an irreconcilable barrier to the development of coherent educational practice.

Skinner

Even more than Thorndike's connectionist psychology, operant learning is characterized by careful management of the external forces (reinforcers) that surround the behaving organism. Learning is most efficient when positive reinforcers are delivered at the moment of behaving. There is no necessity for failure. Failure is the result of a poorly planned program. That is, either the units of behavior are too large or the sequence of reinforcement is inappropriate for the learner.

Skinner would agree with the idealists' views on motivation as being essentially external. The learner is acted on by or responds to forces outside himself. They would also agree that a directive, structured approach to learning is most efficient. Undirected learners accomplish very little. Motivation for both these systems is fundamentally the same. Conflicts about the end goals of society are inherent, but the external means of motivating learners are congruent.

Motivation as produced by forces outside of man is consistent with a realist view of the universe. The best way to advance society is to discover natural law through science and then impart it systematically to the youth of the culture. There is no better way

127

for the realist than through the external objectively sequenced system of programmed operant conditioning. The realist assumes that there is an inherent structure for all bodies of knowledge and disciplines. Breaking structure down into small bits and disseminating it step by step to the learners is a proper way to teach structured knowledge. In his novel outlining a programmed utopian society, Skinner has shown how a form of behavioral engineering could be applied to the control of all aspects of human behavior. Such a society would be self-correcting as more natural law was uncovered by experimental procedures. These laws would be integrated into the core of the scientific society. Skinner's behavioral engineering is an excellent example of one realist's approach toward motivating man to be what he should be through the external control of behavior.

Motivation for the transactive philosophies is personalistic. Arrangement of contingencies of reinforcement as a basic motivational paradigm could not be relevant for the transactionalist unless personal needs and goals were taken into account. Skinnerian psychology pays little attention to internal or personal states except in terms of providing for differential rates of responding and learning. Personal needs are considered mentalistic and are dismissed, leading to an academic and instructional impasse between these positions.

INTERNAL

The Gestaltists

These theorists believe that man is most appropriately viewed as internally motivated. Man behaves in order to reduce perceptual conflicts and to more satisfactorily relate to situations that he perceives as ambiguous. Gestaltists assume that it is part of man's innate nature to attempt to organize and reorganize percepts in order to behave more effectively with relation to the perceived environment.

Perhaps the strongest agreement between idealism and Gestalt psychology is found in the willingness of both groups to posit innate tendencies. In the case of the idealists, however, there

128

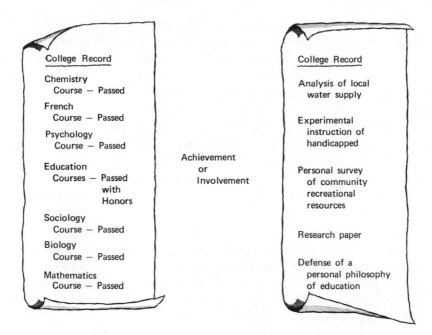

College Record		College Record

Chemistry
  Course — Passed
		Analysis of local
		  water supply

French
  Course — Passed
		Experimental
		  instruction of
		  handicapped

Psychology Course — Passed		

Education
  Courses — Passed
       with
       Honors
	Achievement
	or
	Involvement
		Personal survey
		  of community
		  recreational
		  resources

Sociology Course — Passed		Research paper

Biology
  Course — Passed
		Defense of a
		  personal philosophy
		  of education

Mathematics Course — Passed		

LEARNING: A MATTER OF EMPHASIS.

is more emphasis on the active search by man's mind to live in better harmony with absolute truth or absolute mind. Gestaltists would ignore properties of "mind" and "will" in favor of specifying tendencies to reduce ambiguity and to seek patterns or configurations in perceptions of the environment.

Since Gestalt psychologists tend toward a relativistic view of man's functioning in his universe, they would have difficulty accepting the idealist search for an absolute truth existing outside the individual as the prime motivator. Any view of the world for the Gestaltist is always a subjective interpretation made by the behaver. There would be myriad potential percepts and gestalts to serve as internal motivations for an individual. For the learner these would be functionally adequate and, inevitably, unique to some degree. Such a position obviates agreement with idealism, which assumes motivation to be the search for the ideal percept that lies outside the self.

Gestaltists would say that from a motivational standpoint the

129

person's perceptions determine his behavior rather than what is objectively real in the environment. For the realist motivation is something done to a person, which moves him toward mastery of more natural law. For the Gestaltist the person is internally motivated by his perceptual organization. Problems he perceives will be more significant than those that "objectively" might be more important to an outside observer. Helping the person to perceive new problems to be solved in order to increase his knowledge and intellectual capacity would be acceptable to the Gestaltist. Rejected, however, would be the realist idea that there is one structure of knowledge and therefore one "right" sequence in which learning should naturally occur.

The transactionalists believe that the individual is in some dynamic milieu in which he is a significant figure and the Gestaltists assume that the source of motivation comes from the individual's perceptions. They are both relativistic in their conceptualization of the nature of reality. There is a high degree of congruence between these two systems.

Combs and Snygg

Phenomenologically man is motivated by the internal need to maintain and enhance the self as perceived. The phenomenologist believes that man behaves in terms of what is real to him and what is related to his self at the moment of action. What is actually "out there" is not a central issue. Rather, it is the person's interpretation of reality and its perceived effect on the self-system that motivates all of one's behaving. Although one's needs are all self-related, the self-concept is linked inseparably to personal percepts of the physical and social world in which one lives. Motivation is a transactive process in which interpretations of the universe define problems to which one responds. These interpretations and definitions in turn alter both one's perceptions of self and the universe. A motivated man is always caught up in the process of definitions, solution, redefinition, and resolution of the self in relation to the perceived universe.

Perceptual psychology finds little in common with the idealist line of thought beyond the notion that for both man is more than an empty organism. For the phenomenological psychologist motivation is something other than active search for an external end. Man is a maker of ends and means, who searches for personal truth. The perceptual assumption that ends-means (motivation) are relative to personal constructs of self and society is antithetical to the idealist position of absolutism.

The natural law concept of truth and reality is incompatible with phenomenology. Perceptual psychology accepts the principle that behavior is lawful as do all sciences. To reject the idea that behavior is lawful is to say that there can be no science of human behavior. However, the normative approaches of the realist, which ignore the motivational qualities of individual perceptions, are not adequate for the phenomenologist. Such an individualistic approach to the study of motivation is not relevant to the objectively oriented realists.

In a transactionalist view of the universe man is not separate from his environment; he is integrated with his world. This is a fundamental concept for phenomenological psychology.

It is important to recognize that the perceptual psychologist stresses that the "person" is the "psychological self" or the person as he conceives himself at that moment. Whatever is self-related at a particular time will serve as a motivational function for the behaver. As a person grows psychologically, his self enlarges to include more of the universe. What at one time may have been external and unrelated may at another time be perceived as crucial to the maintenance of self. Although the source of motivation is internal, a growing person does not remain narcissistically self-centered. The transactive motivational dimensions of behavior are in a constant state of flux with a general movement toward increased complexity. This is highly consistent with the idea of the motivation of the mature man being a movement toward a more complex, generous self espoused by the transactional philosophies.

LEARNING: PRODUCT VERSUS PROCESS

Either one of two basic aspects of the learning situation can be given priority by the educator in assessing the validity of an educational experience. For one type of educator the essence of the experience is found in what is learned. The success or failure of the experience is derived from the end product, which is usually available for measurement and evaluation. How much was learned? What score was achieved? What skills were manifested in the final assessment? For another type of educator the essence of the experience is found in the dynamics of the process of learning. Learning is seen as an occurring event and not as an event that has occurred. The relevant questions for evaluation in this case must be related to the qualitative rather than quantitative. Evaluations are predicated on the assessment of a continuing process. What is the student doing? Why is he doing it? How is he dealing with a changing interpretation of the problem? How is he learning to perceive related problems? What evidences of creativity and innovation are evolving from the experience?

In neither case does the educator ignore the secondary aspect. The product-oriented educator is aware that there is a process involved, but it represents only a means to an end. The process-oriented educator recognizes that any number of static ends may serve to generate the critical learning process. He would reject any goal end that did not involve the "good" means.

PRODUCT

Thorndike

In the connectionism of Thorndike the pattern of connections or final pattern of responses is defined as the *sine qua non* of learning. Until the pattern of learning is complete, the learning experience is incomplete and has no more merit than any other good intention. The worth of teaching-learning activities is derived solely from a judgment of how well the end has been achieved. If this goal has been met then the teaching-learning activity was an effective one. If it has not been met then, regardless of the other qualities of the intervening experience, it must be abandoned for something that will promote the end selected.

The idealists emphasize a knowledge of absolute truth, which is an end product of a learning experience. The goodness of a classroom activity is derived from the amount of absolute truth the student possesses after the experience. Since the value of the means is determined by the ends, the ends or products of learning assume paramount importance for the idealists.

To this extent an idealist could adopt Thorndikian teaching-learning concepts and use them in directing learners to all of the "good" ends that the instructor knows.

The realists assume the same mode of thought in the ends-means relationships. Their ends are natural law instead of absolute truth, but they too judge the value of the means by the extent to which it approximates the ends. Science and its methods have become respected by the realists not because of the intrinsic value of the system but because the system has led to discovery of more natural law than any other system of inquiry.

The realist, with his emphasis on the physical science model as a means of discovering more natural law, would find no difficulty in accepting Thorndike's product orientation for education.

The transactionalists do not take an opposite view on the ends-means relationship but transform the issue by stating that means and ends cannot be divided without misinterpreting the whole of human experience. Man thinks and acts in terms of his present situation. Reflections on what has been or will be are made in the present. If man does live in the present moment then what he is doing is done now for the mandates of this moment. The process of learning is an amalgamation of a way to do things and a thing to be done. Thorndike's commitment to product suggests an irreconcilable breech between his position and that of the transactional philosophers.

Skinner

In defining a reinforcer as that which reinforces and in advocating techniques that promote behavior modification toward specified ends, Skinner has clearly indicated his dedication to a product-oriented educational system. Only those processes (schedules of reinforcement) that have been proven to be effective in producing the product (patterns of behavior) are maintained in the repertoire of teaching techniques (programs).

Although Skinner is not an idealist, his system could be used to promote the discovery of absolute truth. To the extent that one knows what absolute truth is, and what has to be done to understand it, one could arrange a series of experiences for the young. One could teach them either the absolute truths discovered by others or how to live in accord with truth. Some could even be taught how to discover absolute truth for themselves. Since the discovery of truth is most often facilitated by an analysis and extrapolation of the truth that others have found, it should be possible to program the experience.

The realists assume that a trained man making systematic observation and analysis under the proper conditions will eventually extend our knowledge of natural law. The ends served are the same ones endorsed by Skinner.

This is one of the cases where a theory of learning has been derived from and within a philosophical system. This does not suggest that the theory is a philosophical extrapolation, but rather that Skinner has not extrapolated his findings or defined his studies beyond the limits imposed by the philosophical system he accepts. Programmed instruction is consistent with realist philosophy and operant conditioning theory, and as such it is a model educational practice.

The transactionalists insist that learning is an evolving process in which the desirable activities (ends-means) depend on the personal-social interpretations made by the individual at the time of acting. They would find little satisfaction or relevance in using Skinnerian theory designed to accomplish a preconceived pattern of behavior selected by someone other than the learner.

The conflict between the product expectation of Skinner and the dynamic flexibility of product-process of the transactionalists leaves almost no room for a synthesis that would not destroy both in the process.

134

PROCESS

The Gestaltists

Problem solving is a process that involves the reorganization of perceptions. The relationships between problems and their solutions are interactive in that the way a problem is solved depends on the way it is perceived. A problem also is defined in part by the means with which we have to solve it. The "rightness" of a solution is a function of who is perceiving and solving the problem. Any of a number of solutions or resolutions may have equal validity as long as the process reduces the ambiguity for the individual learner.

The products of learning are almost incidental to the process except as they indicate an effective learning process has been used. Fixed or prescribed answers are not the essential ingredients of a successful learning experience.

The idealists in their search for known end products of learning (absolute truth) would have some difficulty in using a learning theory in which a personal discovery of a personal solution to a personally perceived problem is the vital operation in education.

Problem solving and experimental approaches are of course the stock in trade of the realists and both are essentials in the learning process for the Gestaltists. However, the reason for the use of these operations generates some questions about the compatibility of the two conceptual models. The philosophy calls for the discovery of natural law (a fixed goal) using a discovery method (scientific method). No particular conflict is generated until one makes the goal of education that of teaching one to discover answers to personally perceived problems.

In this case the end result is dependent on the dynamic processes of the perceiver and the resolutions are functions of the perceiver and his perceptual processes. Only by distorting natural law as being that which satisfies the needs of the perceiver may one force a relationship between realism and Gestalt theory.

The interactive process-product formulation of the transac-

tional philosopher establishes the centrality of a dynamic interpretation of the interrelatedness of action and purpose.

The Gestalt school makes an identical statement in suggesting
that what we are perceiving determines the problems we define.
The problems we define in turn affect our perceptions to the
point that a problem does not have a functional existence except
as we are relating to it.

Transactional philosophy and Gestalt theory assign a relativistic characteristic to the end-means, product-process parame-
ter. The congruence is so complete as to establish an identity
relationship.

Combs and Snygg

Learning is a process of discovering one's personal relationship to and with people, things, and ideas. This process results in
and from a differentiation of the phenomenal field of the individual.

In the associationistic theory mathematical facts, theorems,
and their uses become the end of the study of mathematics. In
Gestalt one attempts to improve one's perceptions of mathematics. For Combs and Snygg one becomes a mathematician by
perceiving one's own relationship to mathematical concerns as a
personal one.

The differentiation process is a never-ending one. The solution of a simple problem enables and engenders the formulation
of more involved problems, which demand more involved
solutions.

A child's questioning procedure illustrates the ever imploding
dynamics of a phenomenological evolvement.

> "What is that?"
> "Grass."
> "What color is it?"
> "Green."
> "What makes it green?"
> "Chemicals."
> "What chemicals?"

"Maybe it's chlorophyll."
"Is chlorophyll green?"
"I don't know. Maybe."
"What makes it green if it is?"

Most parents would run out of answers and patience at about the same time but the child would probably go on for an hour if he were permitted to do so. The answers to the questions asked, to the extent that they were increased differentiations, resulted in not only the solution of the original problem but in the forming of a new, more difficult question. As long as learning is involved in a situation this process continues.

Learning, knowledge, and intelligence are better indicated by the problems being investigated than by the information one has stored or the questions one has asked in the past. The old punch line, "It's not what you've got; it's how you're using it!" clearly states the significant dimensions of the human experience for Snygg and Combs.

Absolute truth is not a function of the perceived need system of the individual. As an end product of education it transcends the personal needs and abilities of most people.

The quest for ultimate mind using personalistic techniques could result only in myriad interpretations of truth none more valid than any other.

The idealists are compelled to reject all systems that make truth and knowledge anything except an absolute end.

The realists have a similar difficulty with this theory. In assuming that truth exists in the process of social sharing, the phenomenological psychologists deny the essence of natural law. The ultimate purpose cannot be to know natural law if the process is to understand one's self in relationship to things that have phenomenological existence. The personalistic phenomena and methodology simply do not relate to the study of the immutable laws of nature.

Transactive philosophy and phenomenological psychology assume that a process-product fragmentation is possible only by sophistic semantic separation. Both define a process experience as one taking place at the moment of action. Neither posit predetermined products in the educational operation.

137

CONGRUENT PHILOSOPHIES AND THEORIES

The congruence of process-product postulates is so complete that it calls for continuing investigation by educators who accept a transactive philosophy of education.

THE TEACHER'S PURPOSE: FIXED VERSUS RELATIVE ENDS

In the formal or planned learning experience, which for this discussion includes experimental laboratory investigations of learning, much attention has been paid to the role of the instructor. All theories agree that learning is the function of the learner, but there are marked differences in what each theory expects of the teacher. Some expect the teacher to have the students achieve some particular predetermined level of competency or skill. Some expect the teaching emphasis to be placed on the development of self and social awareness. Each of the philosophies also imposes certain obligations and responsibilities on the edu-

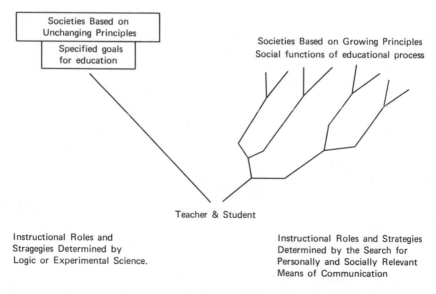

TEACHERS' ROLE: DETERMINED OR DEVELOPING.

cator, which must be taken into account before wedding a theory and a philosophy.

FIXED ENDS

Thorndike

Since learning is connecting and the learner responds mechanistically to stimuli, the elements of the learning experience must be ordered and evaluated by someone other than the learner.

The instructor has the responsibility for determining which lesson (learning experience) is sequentially correct for the learner. He must have the lesson analyzed into a series of logical steps of the size appropriate for the student. Next he is required to present the lesson step by step. He must present the sequentially right stimulus at the right time. When the correct response is made, a reward which the learner accepts must be given. The stimulus, response, reward sequence is presented through a series of elaborations until the learner meets the performance criteria of the instructor.

The total obligation for the management of the experience falls on the shoulders of the teacher who cannot delegate this responsibility to the student.

The search for ultimate truth and absolute mind suggests immediately the folly of letting an immature person assume the responsibility of planning his own educational experience. Truth is usually found after a long and complicated process involving rigorous academic and personal discipline. Neither experience is natural. They are not functions of primitive immature men. The means of discovering truth are fixed by the end: absolute truth. To permit the young to explore methods of inquiring is to permit the repetition of inadequate techniques that have already been tried and discarded by man and society.

The task of finding truth is the most complex and difficult adventure of man. Each individual makes only the smallest of contributions to that knowledge in a disciplined productive lifetime of inquiry. The moral and effective management of education must be done by those who know how to teach the process of discovering truth.

Thorndike's theory provides the basis for a methodology in which the ends and means responsibility and privilege, as in idealism, is reserved for the instructor to use for the benefit of the individual and society.

The method of scientific inquiry is the application of a tried, tested, and true procedure for the discovery of natural law. The extension of knowledge of that law is brought about by use of the methods of science in the study of current problems. Method is not subject to individual review. The scientific method has been validated by decades of investigation. It stands beyond the limits of subjective acceptance or rejection by the young.

Students must be taught the method of step-by-step analysis and the application of predetermined criteria if they are to become technologists. A student is free to say in what area he will extend our understanding of natural law only after he is proficient in the content and method of science in that area as we now know it.

The logical step-by-step development of learning toward a determined end is in all points compatible with realism. It will continue to be so until a more precise knowledge of natural law invalidates Thorndike's description of learning.

Learning is characterized as an individual process of sharing problem definition and solution with others by the transactional philosophies. The imperative of accepting the problems of the individual in his social setting as basic material of education violates the descriptions explicit in Thorndikian theory. The individual cannot be both mechanistic and cognitive. One cannot honor both a logical step-by-step method and the process of personalistic investigation of unique personal problems and meanings. One cannot direct the learner step by step and at the same time hold him accountable for participation in the planning and execution of the learning activity.

Facilitation of the learning process has to be something other than the erudite management of a sequentially sound approximation of predetermined content. The conflict is beyond resolution.

Skinner

Learning is most definitively described as a reassortment of responses. The process is essentially one of random behavior being molded one element at a time until a selected pattern evolves. The subject of this manipulation process is not presumed to be responsible for the selection of the program, its execution, or his responses to it. The total responsibility of the learner is to be available and responsive. Even this is a secondary function of the appropriateness of the programmed material and the effectiveness of the reinforcers selected by the instructor. All complex educational functions are extensions of the basic response-reinforcement paradigm.

Although the idealists have not posited randomness of behavior they have recognized the inherently ineffective behavior of the nondirected learner. Some minor methodological differences would occur if one were to press the distinction between emitted and elicited behavior to its ultimate.

Skinner is committed in operant conditioning to selecting the program (which could be the search for absolute truth) and then waiting until the first "right" behavior is emitted. Whether the idealist would accept the idea that the program limits serve as an adequate motivation or whether they would have a tendency to tell the student what response to make can only be inferred from such general concepts as the socratic dialogue.

The basic agreement that the student must progress from *A* to *B* and that the instructor is responsible for the management and evaluation of the educational program is obvious. The secondary and essential receptive role of the student is also shared.

In general, any differences in teacher behavior between Skinnerian theory and idealism seem to be so minor as to have little if any negative impact on a fruitful union of the two schemes.

The realist's concern for the discovery of natural law is not in conflict with Skinner's formulation since all ends are determined. The discovery of natural law, furthermore, is the ultimate end for Skinner. His search is for the "real" laws of human behavior, which exist independent of theoretical or philosophical bias.

The orderly (scientific) steps in Skinner's programs are de-

141

rived from the application of the scientific method and knowledge of scientific truth (natural law) to the problems of education.

The ends, means, and techniques of realism and Skinner are completely congruent. The educational practices derived from their concatenation are a powerful force in education for the ends selected.

For the same reasons that the transactional philosophers are unable to accept Thorndike they are unable to resolve their differences with Skinnerian constructions. One cannot promote individualized self-other experiences with their cognitive mentalistic overtones using objective bit-by-bit presentations of subject matter. The dynamics of transactive education cannot be prescribed or planned before the event. No one individual has the wisdom to prechoose the "right" or effective behaviors for another.

The fundamental conflict between Skinner ends and means behavior and transactive ends-means behavior precludes for teachers any conjoint use of the two schemes.

RELATIVE ENDS

The Gestaltists

The great emphasis placed on perception and, therefore, personal organizations in learning creates a rather complicated relationship between the instructor and the student.

Unfortunately for the simplification of the problem, the field theorists do not support the obverse of the associationists' position. The student is not the sole independent adjudicator of educational practice or outcome. He must be involved in the experience and yet he cannot be the "all" of the experience. The congruence of the perceptions of the individual and the problem he considers as the content of education must be maintained. Neither subservience to predetermined goals or methodologies, nor complete delegation of responsibility by the teacher meets the demands of the Gestalt theory. Doing what he "wants" to do is no better than doing what he is told to do. The ends-means of Gestalt learning is found in doing those things the student discovers he "needs" to do.

The teacher's role in the discovery of personal need is that of promoting a learning situation in which the learner develops and maintains a broad personal perspective. His perspective must include the perceptions of others as well as his private interpretations.

The difficult task of facilitation for the Gestalt instructor is to cause the student to enlarge his perceptions to include salient features of the world of things and others. The teacher must introduce ideas and experiences that are contrary to the limited closed perceptual systems of the contented uninformed. This agitation must not be done in any way that would cause the student to feel he was bad, ignorant, or irresponsible for holding his earlier perception.

During the process of reorganization the educator continues his active critical support by expecting and asking the learner to explain, substantiate, and document the validity of his new perceptual organizations.

The relative ends-means relationship involved in perceptual reorganization presumes the validity only of such material as can be identified as personally meaningful by the learner.

The idealists would not expect a teacher to help a student discover a personal subjective interpretation of ultimate truth. First, most individuals are incapable of rising above their own stations high enough to gain the perspective required to find truth. Second, truth is related to the eccentricities of the personal experience in such small amounts and such obscure ways as to obviate the validity of such expectations.

The ideal teacher would be expected to present logical material as a model for the student's search for truth. The methods and materials have to support the idea of an ultimate reality beyond the personal experience.

A teacher trying to facilitate both Gestalt theory and idealism would be serving two masters equally poorly.

Realism's emphasis on objectivity, the denial of the subjective experience, and the search for extant ends using specified means would create an unfathomable quandary if it were imposed as the end of a personal, perceptual organization process.

This dilemma has escaped many teachers who predicate extensive curricula in which students learn to discover what the teacher has planned for them to discover. Discovery techniques developed and used extensively by the Gestaltists engender their validity as Gestalt techniques when used in the dynamic ends-means process as described above.

The interactive philosophies, if anything, go beyond the Gestalt theorists in their support of the teacher's role as being that of critically supporting the growth of the young in the educational situation.

The validity of an interpretation for an individual is derived from his sincerity and diligence in investigating the basis for his attitude. The educator presses the individual to meet his personal-social obligations in understanding and acting on the premises he postulates for himself. The responsibility of interjecting new ideas and experiences and questioning the learner about his process-product are not only accepted but demanded of the transactive teacher.

Combs and Snygg

Further differentiation of the phenomenological field occurs as an individual recognizes some inadequacy of a present organization. When a change is needed to maintain or enhance the phenomenal self, it is made by the individual as the right and proper thing to do. This process is not always an aware one fully entered into by the learner. The role of the educator is to facilitate the process. Often this is done by presenting situations in which the learner may come to see the need for involvement. In his participation the educator asks the person to evaluate or to justify approaches or outcomes. A critical attitude to be developed is that behavior should be available for sharing. More than to prove the learner is right or to catch him in error, critical inquiry by the teacher should be interpreted by the learner as a chance to meet his privilege-obligation of shared social intercourse — to share his experience-interpretations with as many people as are interested in sharing.

The phenomenological goal in teaching is an expansion of phenomenological self to incorporate a multiplicity of people, objects, and ideas. The end of the experience is synonymous with the means of the experiencing. Differentiation, growth, or expansion are indeterminate terms indicating dynamic evolvements.

The teacher's role is to encourage an attitude of personal adequacy in spite of an environment forever in a state of flux moving in unanticipated directions.

The personal-social relativism of the Snygg and Combs interpretation, with its reliance on the truth as perceived at the moment of experience, places the whole system apart from an idealistic philosophy.

Sharing of knowledge for the idealists occurs between equals, not between the knowledgeable and the ignorant. The giving of knowledge to the uninformed promotes movement toward the ultimate end, but permitting the questioning of the known, using personal perceptions as the reference point, is not consistent with the purpose of promoting the "good" education.

The effective teacher in a realist system is charged with the promotion of a student's movement towards his acceptance or discovery of natural law. With the ends fixed, the degrees of freedom of the means are restricted to those activities that cause or permit such movement.

The role of the teacher cannot be to honor and respect the personal values, judgments, and experiences of the individual and at the same time to exert pressure in moving him toward fixed ends using tested means.

The endogenerative nature of motivation and values is congruent with neither the ends nor means of realism. Any forced union of this theory and philosophy can result only in a distortion of the basic premise of one or both.

If the purpose of education is to cause a constant reassessment of self and society in a never-ending growth experience, then the role of the teacher has to be that of encouraging self-discovery, the development of social awareness, and the skills of social criticism. Ends are understood but unfixed, and means are functions of personal interpretation. Ends and means are dynamically interrelated. All of education becomes a matter of sharing thoughts about a changing universe. The sharing of personal universes by kindergarten children is as valid for them as

145

the dialogues of Nobel laureate physicists. The theory of differentiation with its personalistic assumptions fits into the relativistic frame of reference of transactionalism. The teacher's role is to help the student to determine his own best way of solving problems of which he is aware in such ways as to meet his needs and support others serving other ends.

LEARNING CAPACITY: QUANTITATIVE VERSUS QUALITATIVE

No modern psychological theory sets a specific limit on physical capacity of persons for learning. However, within a framework of nonspecific limits there are tendencies toward viewing the human being as either mechanical or a dynamic organism. On the whole, the associationists favor a mechanical approach, although the field psychologists favor a relativistic evolutionary dynamic view of man's capacity.

CAPACITY: LEVELS OF DESCRIPTION (NORMATIVELY— EIGHT OUNCES OF WATER; FUNCTIONALLY—EXTENSION OF LIFE).

The major philosophical systems discussed in this text favor positions ranging from a rather highly fixed view of man's capacity for idealists to an essentially open-ended systems approach for the transactionalists. Comparison of the various psychological theories and philosophical schools reveals strong compatabilities and conflicts among various combinations of systems.

146

Quantitative Approaches

Thorndike

The basis of intelligence in this theory is the number of S-R bonds or connections that are available to an organism. When an animal reaches maturity the neural structure becomes stable and the ultimate capacity or potential for making S-R bonds becomes fixed. Even within a fixed framework, however, it is almost always possible to increase the number of S-R bonds actually formed by effective manipulation of rewards. Intelligence, in Thorndike's view, is largely a quantitative matter measured in terms of the number of S-R connections that an organism can exhibit, not the number of connections he may make someday.

The idealist can accept Thorndike's view of ultimate capacity as being fixed. The agreement ends here. The idealists do not accept the quantitative notion of individual differences. Men are subdivided into classes or types on the basis of qualitative differences. Those who have the qualitative power to contemplate aspects of absolute mind have better capacity than men who are workers or laborers. Liberal education for the liberal man is reserved for those who can best engage in higher thought processes. Not all men can profit from a liberal education. Some men are destined inevitably to be workers and some others are capable of becoming thinkers. These differences are due to innate qualities. Such an approach is not compatible with Thorndike's quantitative model of human capacity.

Thorndike's mechanical, additive conception of intelligence as a quantitative dimension is highly consistent with a realist view of capacity. Realists liken the body to a machine—a complex one to be sure—which has controls not unlike a computer to direct its parts. The amount of intelligence an organism may possess is determined by the complexity of the computer (brain) that exists. The whole machine including the complex computer functions according to natural laws. As man uncovers these natural laws, he will be able to discern more and more atomistic levels of operation of the brain. The S-R bond concept is a satisfactory starting point. It may well be that ultimately much of S-R bond theory may be

147

explained in terms of electrochemical or other quantitative aspects of the brain.

Transactionalists find Thorndike's notion of intelligence unacceptable. Thorndike makes capacity too much a closed system. There is little room for continual evolution to states of *new* equilibrium as man encounters and attempts to solve new problems. For the transactionalist, man is purposive. The reactive approach characteristic of connectionism measured in quantitative units is a static concept that cannot account adequately for innovative qualitative behavior of human beings.

Skinner

Physiological limits of capacity are of little concern in operant conditioning theory. Skinner is much more concerned with accurate assessment of the present level of functioning of an organism. This is necessary in order that an appropriate program or schedule of operant conditioning can be selected for use in further development of more complex behavior. Skinner is exclusively concerned with an external behavioral approach. He prefers not to posit intervening qualitative variables that must be inferred rather than directly observed. His preference is for external quantitative assessment of the learner's performance level. Skinner suggests that all species and individual differences are matters of quantitative differences in response rates.

The idealist's notion of the endowment of mind is inconsistent with a quantitative Skinnerian theory. A psychological theory that omits constructs of mental operations, qualitative differences of various classes of people, and transcendental functions is unacceptable to a philosophy concerned with the approximation of ultimate mind and absolute truth.

Skinner and realist philosophy are in close agreement on learning limits. Both define mental operations in physical terms; both accept natural determinism or natural law; and both reject purposive behavior in human beings.

Ultimately, Skinner avoids the issue of cortical capacity via his completely external approach to viewing the behavior of organisms. By behavior he means observable elements of overt action or reaction by the organism in a physically described environment. This is acceptable to the realists, since it avoids the problem of positing qualitative states of the organism that are impossible to define and measure quantitatively. Basically realists assume that intelligence exists—in some specific amount—and that the amount of intelligence can be measured. If this is proven false, then new, more efficient, objective, physical descriptions of capacity will ultimately be uncovered leading to precise prediction and control of the natural components of intelligence.

Skinner and transactionalism agree that measurement of biological limits is not crucial at present in the development of science. This agreement occurs on different grounds. As stated earlier Skinner is more concerned with shaping behavior as a quantitative change in the response rate of the organism. Transactionalists on the other hand assume that intelligence is a constantly changing function of a qualitative situation. They also assume that intelligence is specific to the individual. Therefore, it is probably impossible to quantify either capacity or intelligence. Normative measures or "tests" of capacity satisfactory for one person would rarely be satisfactory for another, since humans are all unique and have different views of the universe.

QUALITATIVE APPROACHES

The Gestaltists

Intelligence is the ability to act with foresight or to behave effectively when confronted with problems that are unique in personal experience. Intelligence is not exclusively a matter of physiology and anatomy. Biological factors are significant only as they relate to the ability to differentiate and restructure percepts. A person who is able to confront and solve new problems and sees himself as capable of resolving ambiguity in new situations is intelligent. Differences in intelligence are not the number of things done but the ways in which they are done.

Idealists would find the Gestaltists' viewpoint on the issue of

149

learning limits at odds with theirs. For the Gestaltist, facilitation of the development of insight and new ways of solving unique problems are central. The idealists' notion that all that exists is "already there" in the world of ideas just waiting to be contemplated or known is not acceptable. Verbal facility in manipulating known truth may give the idealist some adequate measure of a person's intelligence or capacity, but this would be inadequate for the Gestaltist. The agreement between the two groups that capacity is qualitative is minor in comparison to the disagreement on man's potential for growth and development.

The realist view of potential as objective and absolute is in conflict with Gestalt theory. The relativistic bent of the Gestaltist is not in tune with the realist's notion of the universe as fixed and operating according to natural laws that can be uncovered. The Gestaltist sees problems as always unique to the learner — the learner will perceive in terms of his view of the problem at hand. Such an individualistic approach is not reconcilable with the objective, normative scheme of the realist.

Gestalt psychology and transactive philosophies are in general harmony regarding capacity. Neither is concerned primarily with measuring what "capacity" is so much as facilitating each individual's potential for problem solving. Man is fixed for neither group. He is in a state of flux or constant metamorphosis. Man is always involved in developing more and more complex perceptions. This is a continuous process throughout life. Men exist in communion with each other, but they are all unique. They can share parts of others' percepts and problems, but they are not stamped from identical molds. Intelligence is inferred from the qualitative dimensions of behavior for both groups.

Combs and Snygg

These phenomenologists have made perhaps the strongest and most direct statements of any theorists discussed here on the problem of maximal limits of behavior. Combs and Snygg posit that the limits of what any particular person might perceive seem nonexistent for all practical purposes. Given a healthy organism, positive environmental influences, and a nonrestrictive set of percepts of self there appears to be no foreseeable end to the perceptions possible for the individual. This is clearly the most open-ended statement of dynamic capacity encountered among the respective theorists.

The view of man's capacity as predetermined and unchanging is antithetical with the perceptual point of view. The mind-body dichotomy that is characteristic of idealist views on mental capacity is also a source of contention. Though the phenomenologist sees man as a purposive being, he is not conceived as having a mind that is a separate force directing the body. Rather, man is purposive in the sense that he attempts perceptually to anticipate problems. This anticipatory thinking affects his perceptions of the present and, ultimately, his acts in the present. A perceptual definition of capacity is not consistent with the idealists' view of man's nature.

Realism supports an external view of man's capacity. Phenomenologically man cannot be described or understood using an exclusively physicalistic, external frame of reference. The normative view of man accepted by the realist is not compatible with the personalistic approach of perceptual psychology. One cannot describe capacity of unique individuals using ounces, pounds, or percentiles. Moreover, the fixed natural law concept of man is inadequate to account for phenomenological interpretations of man and his changing, growing nature and intellectual capacity.

Transactional philosophy and phenomenological theory both accept a relativistic, personal approach toward describing the capacity of man. All men are unique. Therefore, capacity is always stated in idiographic terms. Rather than focus on measuring capacity, which the phenomenologist considers virtually unlimited, there is agreement that a more valid goal is understanding what goes into the development of more adequate persons capable of fuller utilizations of the immense potentialities available in each of us.

TRANSFER: MECHANICAL VERSUS DYNAMIC

A classical question in formal educational circles for years was: "Does learning one thing help you learn something else or must we teach everything from the beginning?"

CONGRUENT PHILOSOPHIES AND THEORIES

After more than fifty years of experimental inquiry the question has been altered. Now it is, "How does learning one thing help you to learn another?"

Just as psychology was able to answer the first question in the affirmative, the multiplicity of psychological approaches and their

(a)   (b)

TRANSFER: IDENTIFICATION OF RELEVANT LEARNING (A) IDENTITY OF ELEMENTS PREVIOUSLY LEARNED AND (B) RELATIVITY OF PERCEPTUAL PATTERNS.

philosophical and methodological differences resulted in different explanations for the commonly accepted phenomena of transfer.

The associationists, with their preference for mechanical models, quite naturally see transfer as a complex extension of an associative process. The field theorists with equal conviction affirm transfer as a process in which dynamic interpretations are modified and are made available for use in new situations.

The philosophies rarely make reference to this aspect of the learning process, but a number of commitments support or fail to support the positions taken by the various theories.

Mechanical

Thorndike

Thorndike's first positive assertion about the existence of transfer was developed within his framework of the S-R connection unit. Since he saw learning as stimulus-response and investigated the more complex learnings with S-R methods and tools, transfer was expressed as an extension of the mechanical S-R model.

152

His first studies resulted in the concept of identical elements. If a person learned situation one with elements *ABC* and then faced situation two with elements *ABD* the learner would have a marked advantage in solving problem number two. Elements *A* and *B* as learned elements could be immediately used without going through another stimulus-response-reward sequence.

Further experimental investigations revealed that not only did identical elements transfer in new learning but that related or similar elements were transferable. If a student learned *ABC* in one situation and was taught that *ABC* was a sequential series and understood how *A* related to *B* and *C*, etc., then when situation two consisted of *DEF* or 123, he was able to solve the problem much more economically. The process permits learning of principles and generalizations that have value beyond that of learning a particular fact.

The idealists generally have adopted an accumulative concept of knowledge. This means that bit-of-truth is added to bit-of-truth. Our present understanding is the product of all we have found of ultimate truth.

Essentially the idealist can accept Thorndike's presentation as a harmonious interpretation of reality. The idealistic process of discovering truth consists of an intensive review of accumulated bits of knowledge for the purpose of finding principles or generalizations that will give a more definitive view of truth. Absolute truth will not negate any valid bit of information. Eventually the manipulation of these bits will result in better comprehension. The philosophers are people who can identify the basic elements of truth and find them in different situations. They are also able to generate a better knowledge of true principles by finding identical and similar elements in a variety of behaviors.

With truth fixed and bits of truth unchanging, no critical differences between Thorndike's scientific formulation and idealism's philosophical description are evident. The process of transfer is inherently congruent regardless of any other dissimilarities that may exist.

The fixed and static natural law of the realist is discovered through an analysis and generalization of the discrete bits of knowledge found by the scientific investigation of any area.

In no case does the addition of all the bits transcend or trans-form natural law. Knowing more facts permits one to make better generalizations. The generalizations are never more than approximations of natural law. Many of the facts we have are the truest statements we have. They may be modified as we discover more of natural law. When we finally determine a true fact it will lead us to other true facts because one bit-of-truth is fixed in its relationship to another bit-of-truth.

The accumulative model and the method of generating principles and generalizations are analogous to Thorndike's transfer prototype.

Interactive philosophies do not accept mechanism as an adequate interpretation of man's functioning. Man's experience does not consist of bits with static autonomies. The dynamic interpretations of behavior preclude any consideration of transfer as an accumulative process no matter how complex and generalized the formulation becomes. Learning is not mechanical because man is not reactive. Transfer has to be something other than a complex mode of associating stimuli and responses.

Skinner

As a variation on a response model Skinner's scheme shows the transfer process developed by Thorndike. Skinner as a latter-day scientists gives much more emphasis to the generalization of responses but does not neglect or minimize the import of identical elements. For Skinner the elements of behavior are reinforced operants and for Thorndike the elements are rewarded connections. Except for this difference, the two theories subscribe to the same description of transfer.

Taken in isolation the transfer process of Skinner is acceptable to the idealist on the same grounds that Thorndike's process is compatible.

With no essential differences between Skinner and Thorndike the realists find the Skinner position as valid and effective as Thorndike's.

The transactionalists reject Skinner for his use of operationalism and non-cognitive constructs to account for human behavior.

DYNAMIC

The Gestaltists

Simple learning is the reorganization of a perceptual pattern. The perceptual configuration is a pulsing, changing, growing interpretation of a complex of relationships.

This interpretation of relationships is developed in a specific situation. The essential question of transfer is: How does previous learning help us to reorganize in the future? Organizations have a quality that goes beyond the specific elements involved in the pattern. The whole is more than the sum of the parts. The wholeness of gestalts are still valid even when specific aspects are altered. An example is that of a melody. A group of differently pitched noises of varying duration can become reorganized into a pattern which we recognize as a melody. Once we "know the tune" it can be transposed and played in different keys. It can be sung, and it can be played on different instruments. Many melodies can be further transposed to march, polka, waltz, and other rhythm patterns without destroying the original identity.

Other learned patterns may also be transposed and dynamically applied to new situations without destroying the original configuration or imposing it on the new problem. The concept of "economy" can be used in simple financial situations to mean that one should buy a given item for the lowest possible price. The concept can be used with equal validity to suggest that one should never invest more effort or time in a project than the result warrants. In many situations involving "economy" one must spend a little more to get a great deal more. In teaching, it may be more economical to teach for transfer in the initial learning than to teach all the possible applications at a later time. One does not have to reteach a hundred variations of the application of the original concept.

Transposition involves qualitative manipulations of perceptions. Quantitative or discrete elements are not directly involved.

155

The idealists accept only a part of transposition. If one accepts truth as fixed and bits of truth as fixed parts of that whole truth, then truth could be transposed from one particular situation to another. At this superficial level there appears to be agreement.

However, it is unfair to distort the relativism of Gestalt by slipping in an assumption that ultimate reality and truth are knowable. The only thing of equal unfairness is to invalidate the basic beliefs of the idealist by interpreting truth as something generated by the individual.

Truth for both systems can be transposed because of the validity of truth and its universality. But truth is not the same thing: It is not discovered by the same process; it does not serve the same ends. Transfer as the use of truth in varying situations has only the most deceptive similarity and may not be used by one teacher to accomplish both ends with any one group.

The realists' differences with Gestalt transposition are even more subtle than are those of the idealists. The Gestalt experiments were done within an experimental mode in which many of the restrictions of the realists were honored. The paradox is not clear until we ask what was so experimentally objectively studied. The answer comes out eventually as the subjective reactions of man. The fact that the reactions were to objective situations, and that some normative and descriptive limits were placed on the studies, does not alter the basic fact that the Gestaltist chose to be concerned with dynamic processes instead of quantitative products in learning. The reality of an experience was found to be in the validity of the experience for the individual. Man is not particularly receptive to or appreciative of natural law. Much of his behavior seems to violate the natural law of the realist who persists in using physical science as a model.

That the whole is more than the sum of the parts and that wholes maintain their integrity even when elements are altered or removed from the situation can only be interpreted by the realist as some sort of metaphysical phenomena neither to be criticized nor considered.

The realist can understand, explain, control, and use transfer of the type presented by Thorndike and Skinner without the alteration of premises required in the endorsement of Gestalt transposition.

The transactional relativism of the systems presented in this volume assume learning to be a unique individual experience. The experience is essentially one of personal interpretation in which factors are not related on a one-to-one or equal-weighted basis. The experience of the individual is always in a process of personal evolution toward indeterminant goals by unique means. That man is aware of previous experiences and uses them in the assessment of the present is accepted. That transfer is a direct application of previous learning is denied.

The use of patterns transposed by the personal experiences of the individual to solve present personal problems fits the transactive circumscriptions imposed on a humanistic description of transfer.

Combs and Snygg

The hallmark of effective learning is not the extent to which a child can talk or write about desirable behavior. Performing a desirable act in the school situation is not the epitome of learning behavior. The most effective criterion for determining whether something learned helps one to learn something else is whether the learner uses the behavior voluntarily in the solution of problems faced in his life situations out of school. One is said to be transferring learning when it is being used outside the situation in which it was learned.

Basic learning is a process of differentiation in which personal relationships are recognized, understood, and modified in such ways as to enhance or to maintain the phenomenal self. Transfer is a matter of taking current differentiations and using them as first approximations in the determination of the relationship of self to new situations. The self-concept is always the central issue in phenomenological interpretations of learning. It is also central to the concept of transfer.

The first approach to a problem probably consists of an admission that one does not know what his relationship to the item at

157

hand is. If one knows his relationship he knows what to do, and the problem is not a problem because there is no ambiguity.

The outcome of the original learning is the self-percept, "I now know what to do in this situation." As a first phase such a statement and its related behavior is to be commended. However, such a statement has little value as an interpretation of successful transfer. The specificity of the statement, if unaltered, will result in either of two inadequate perceptions in new situations. In one case, the response might be, "I know what to do in this situation so I will do the same thing in the new situation!" No two transactive situations have so much identity that transfer can be so direct. The second alternative is equally inefficient because it would lead a person to exaggerate the specificity of his learning. "I know what to do here, but I don't know what to do there." In neither case does the person perceive himself to be an adequate and creative individual confidently attacking a problem in terms of situational demands.

The ultimate of transfer is being achieved when a modest statement of this nature can be made: "I have dealt with this kind of problem before. I was able to solve that one. This problem is enough like what I have done before that I can figure out what I need to do in this situation."

Neither identical nor similar elements or even transposition of patterns adequately account for the dynamics of the personal interpretation of the problem and the transfer behavior related to it.

The form of this type of transfer behavior would appeal to the idealists who would expect the learner to exhibit the confidence and skill reflected in the phenomenological statement of transfer attitude. However, the method used to arrive at this end and the acceptance of this behavior as an end violate the basic assumptions of the philosophy. The end of the search is not for man to master facts or to discover truth for utilitarian purposes. One does not discover truth to solve problems. The discovery of truth is life's problem. The difficulties of life suffered by individuals are due almost entirely to the fact that man has not discovered enough truth or dedicated himself to living in accord with truth. The self-discovery ends-means is too superficial a process for the idealists. Transfer would have to involve ideas beyond those relating to the personal-social relationships of man.

If transfer is a process of taking that part of man's discoveries that have been proven to be real and true, and building approximations of natural law from these bases, then Snygg and Combs have little to offer.

Neither the self-concept nor the sense of adequacy have been operationally defined, normative methods of measurement have not been discovered, and the ends of the process have not been shown to result in the better understanding of natural law. The personalistic approach to transfer leaves little for the realist to admire except the logic of the system. The personalistic assumptions underlying the system preclude its acceptance as an operational model for education.

The transactive imperatives are manifest in three crucial and interrelated aspects of phenomenological transfer: Learning is a unique, personal experience; transfer is a relational transaction between the person and the problem; ends are found in the individual providing himself with ever changing, always improving, and growing means of relating to broader problems.

PERMANENCE OF LEARNING: CONDITIONING VERSUS RELEVANCE

What causes us to remember what we have learned? Is it a matter of the effectiveness of rewards and the proper pairing of stimuli and responses? Is it the degree to which material to be learned is seen as meaningful and relevant from the learner's

(a)   (b)

PERMANENCE OF LEARNING: CONDITIONING OR SITUATIONAL RELEVANCE (A) THE SHAPE OF A FORGED IRON BAR IS FIXED BY PRIOR SHAPING AND (B) BUT THE PERMANENCE OF ITS MAGNETISM IS A FUNCTION OF THE INTERACTION OF A VARIETY OF FORCE FIELDS.

view? Quite possibly the permanence of learning may be affected by all the above factors plus additional contingencies such as level of maturation, fatigue, or other internal states of the organism.

In any case, the general orientation of the associationist regarding permanence in learning is different from that of persons who incline toward a psychological field approach. Associationists accept conditioning as the formation of effective, permanent learning. Humanistic or field psychologists accept personal relevance as the prime factor that influences remembering. Such preferences as these ultimately determine the educational practices of the professional worker.

Conditioning Approaches

Thorndike

In the connectionist's view conditioning occurs through reward of appropriate behavior. It is also assumed that the conditions under which reward is delivered influence the effectiveness of the reward in determining future behaviors to be evoked. Accordingly in their research, connectionists have spent a great deal of time and effort studying the permanence of the conditioning process. Questions of major concern have been: What is the most effective time to present a reward? What is the effect of lack of reward? What are the effects of punishment? What are the effects of practice? The careful control of all contingencies having an impact on the conditioning process is essential to optimal learning and retention.

Permanence of learning is measured by resistance to decay of patterns of behavior that have been stamped in by rewarded practice of appropriate responses.

Although Thorndike's monistic view of the organism is not paralleled by the idealist formulation of ultimate reality as being separate from the world of the sensory being, the reward model could be accepted for the facilitation of permanence of learned symbol manipulation. On the whole, however, the idealist would tend to view all S-R behavior as being sensate and relatively inconsequential. The higher thought processes characteristic of idealistic thinking are apart from the sensate. Such learning as produced by S-R means might be permanent, but unless it increases contemplative powers, difficult to define or measure by objective means, any learning is comparatively insignificant.

Realists are chiefly concerned with the assimilation of factual material and the mastery of bodies of subject matter. In opposition to the idealist, nothing can be known except through the raw material of sensation. Objective study of the real world of existence is paramount. Thorndike's connectionist psychology is likewise concerned with objective measurement of responses in the presence of reward or other conditions. This external, sensate, objective approach has an inherent appeal to realists, since the permanence of learning is defined in units which can be readily counted and measured. Using the connectionist approach enables the educator to quantify the learning experiences of students. The realist teacher, therefore, is able to count the number of correct responses to measure the retention of facts and principles taught by means of the system of rewards. One can objectively measure the number and duration of responses made under certain conditions of reward. Such a direct method of determining the effectiveness of learning is highly congruent with realist philosophy.

The learner-centered approach to education accepted by the transactional philosophies is inconsistent with Thorndike's conditioning approach to permanence of learning. Connectionist rewards are delivered with little concern as to whether the material to be learned is perceived as significant for the behaver. In a sense, the learner does what he does not from any sense of personal identification with the problems of the learning experience but, rather, because he has been rewarded. This separation is comparable to an ends-means separation, which is incompatible with the whole of interactionist philosophy. Permanence as a fixed pattern of externally derived behaviors is equally nontransactive.

Skinner

In operant learning permanence is determined by the management of reinforcers rather than by rewards. For Skinner, schedules of reinforcement are crucial to the permanency or resistance to extinction of a response or group of responses. Fixed schedules produce more susceptibility to extinction than variable schedules of reinforcement. Also of importance is careful step-by-step building up of response chains in programmed sequences of material. A response chain that is not carefully sequenced is more likely to break down than one that has been reduced to sufficiently small elements that permit adequate reinforcement at each step in the learning process.

Equally true for operant conditioning would be the idealist criticism of connectionism. Namely, the idealists conceive of S-R behavior as being rather elemental and simplistic. Presumably operant conditioning could be used to produce some permanence of low-level associations but it would be inadequate for teaching the art of contemplation. Since contemplation of the world of ideas is the only true form of higher learning recognized by the idealists, Skinner's conditioning of physical responses could serve only a rudimentary role.

Realist philosophy with its external and objective approach would embrace operant behavior shaping as a means of facilitating retention. Skinner's penchant for building up large volumes of data on the behavior of organisms is aligned with the realists' notion of objective inquiry. His inductive approach to generating laws governing behavior would also be a source of strong realist support. Thus, it would be most acceptable for the realist to adopt a Skinnerian approach to measure the learning and retention of learning of humans and other animals with quantitative appraisal of overt responses.

Both the model of reinforcement and the step-by-step sequencing of instruction would fit realist philosophical assumptions. Permanence is based on objective criteria, and it follows the realist notion that material has an inherent structure with a temporal dimension that can be quantitatively determined.

The receptacle theory or empty organism approach to learning and retention subscribed to by Skinner is unacceptable to the transactionalists. Interactionist philosophy cannot reconcile a source of reinforcement external to the learner with the internal approach to motivation which it postulates. Neither is an external design of step-by-step sequencing of materials assumed to be adequate for the individual learner. As external sources of reinforcement are rejected, so is the Skinnerian proposition that permanence is a function of the rigor of the pattern in which such reinforcement is administered.

RELEVANCE

The Gestaltists

Organization of perceptions in meaningful ways and understanding of relevant principles of problem solution are crucial to permanence of learning. Meaningfully understood learnings are applicable to a larger body of problems and, therefore, remain in use longer. Utilizing external rewards rather than internal sources of motivation is not effective in facilitation of meaning or in long-term memory. It is only as percepts are structured or restructured in a personally relevant learning experience that the process will result in formation of lasting memory trace systems. Even so, trace systems are not static, but are always being transformed through interaction with new learning processes. Drill and repetition, whether rewarded or unrewarded, are not as productive in producing "permanent" learnings as is meaningful insight learning following motivated searching, trying, and reorganizing activities.

The idealist view of the goal of education, as absorption in absolute truth found in the world of ideas, suggests that the ultimate source of permanence of learning is a universal one found outside the learner. The only knowledge of any lasting value for man is external to the behaver — ideas.

Facilitating personal and unique perception structures is antagonistic to idealism. The traditionalist cannot accept what the Gestaltist requires for a significant learning experience with strong trace systems: that is, insight derived from a personal search for meaning in a real world of existence.

The conceptualization of man as a machine is embraced by realists. This leads to a view of permanence of learning which can only accept a quantitative approach to remembering. The realists' spectator view of man holds that man is an object that reacts to forces in the natural environment. The real physical world is the only objective reality. Hence, to produce permanent learning and to measure its permanence is an objective, mechanical task rooted in the physical world of existence. A unique insight or perception structure is inconsistent with realist assumptions. Knowing is found exclusively in sense perceptions. The realist searches for common sensations of men in arriving at what is, should be, or can be known. An objective and external approach to permanence as a biological function cannot be reconciled with the Gestalt notion of permanence of trace systems as unique, personal, changing dynamisms in each organism.

The transactional view of knowledge with its postulation of learner-centeredness identifies personal and internal motives as enabling permanent meaningful learning. This is in harmony with the Gestaltist position that organizing perceptions in ways seen as relevant by the behaver produces strong trace systems.

A further source of agreement is found in the shared idea that for these systems perception of relationships between parts and whole, means and ends facilitates useful, valid, and reliable persistent perceptions.

Combs and Snygg

Learning tasks that are understood as self-related are accepted as problems to be solved. This internal identification of self with learning problem facilitates the rate of learning and availability of what has been learned under internally motivated conditions. For the phenomenologists people are always motivated. That is, a learner will do that which is necessary to effectively maintain and enhance the self. The conditions of motivation promote meaningful learning. Those problems that are "real" to the behaver are resolved as ambiguity is reduced. Stable concepts are those that continue to be relative to the solution of personal problems. Self-related learning persists. It is integrated into new perceptual patterns and is in flux as necessary to meet the exigencies of living. As a dynamic it is not fixed but changes as the self grows throughout life.

The best way to foster permanent learning is to learn that which is absolute, fixed, and forever correct. This for the idealist is the world of ideas which is independent of personal meaning. Phenomenologists consider permanent learning to be that which is personally meaningful and relevant to the self as perceived. The idealists have little regard for the permanence of self-related learnings.

The assimilation of facts and mastery of knowledge accepted as basic by the realists predisposes that school of thought to an external view of development of permanency in learning. Permanency is fostered and measured by objective means. Knowing is only illustrated through the medium of overt measurable responses. Responding to stimuli is an overt sign of knowledge, which exists in the nervous system of the organism. The organism is a receptacle into which knowledge is placed. Permanency of retention is tested by drawing off samples of this knowledge and comparing it with what was taught and with what others in an equivalent normative group can report. Personal involvements of the learner and meaningfulness of learning are not relevant for the realist, producing a conflict with perceptual theory.

Transactionalists and phenomenologists agree that permanence of learning is related to personalistic validity. Transactive philosophies hold that the educational experience should be constructed to be learner centered. For the field psychologist, problems must be self-related. In neither case are problems generated by external manipulators and handed to learners. Central to these systems is the question of how to develop learning experiences that will continue to facilitate the need to explore and the search for new answers for problems that are personal to the learner. Learning is permanent to the extent that it generates problems that may be shared by others and to the degree that continued sharing itself is enhancing. Both systems agree that unless the learner sees the issue at hand as significant for him, there would be little reason to expect that permanent learning would result.

PRIMARY SOURCES FOR FURTHER READING

Combs, Arthur W. *The Professional Education of Teachers.* Boston: Allyn and Bacon, 1965.

Combs, Arthur W., et al. *Florida Studies in the Helping Professions.* Gainesville: U. of Florida Press, 1969.

Skinner, B. F. *Walden Two.* New York: Macmillan, 1948.

SECONDARY SOURCES AND COLLECTIONS OF READINGS

Bigge, Morris L. "A Relativistic Approach to the Learning Aspect of Educational Psychology." *Educational Theory,* July 1964, pp. 213–220.

Evans, Richard I. *B. F. Skinner: The Man and His Ideas.* New York: Dutton, 1968.

Kuenzli, Alfred E. *The Phenomenological Problem.* New York: Harper and Row, 1959.

Morris, Van Cleve. *Philosophy and the American School.* Boston: Houghton Mifflin, 1961.

SET FIVE

Rational Educational Practice

OBLIGATORY PREROGATIVES

Both associative and field models have their merits, but one cannot value both of them equally without creating an inconsistent practice. Some contemporary educators are attempting to resolve the issue of consistency by proclaiming all theories to be inadequate and all philosophies to be semantic snares. They then proceed to teach on a day-by-day basis using whatever technique strikes their fancy at the moment. Such notions may promote education as an art but do not promote it as a profession. For us rational educational practice demands a consistency of practice with the related continuity of experience for the learner. Illogical union of theory and philosophy or denial of theory and/or philosophy has yet to generate an effective coherent public education practice.

At some point in the development of a personal professional educational practice, the educator must close his books and rely on his own interpretations. What he should do in the classroom cannot be specified by theory or philosophy, or left to visceral machinations. Only general guidelines can be derived from these

167

abstractive sources. An individual or a group responds to the teacher and what he does, not what he hopes to do. The teacher's task is to translate theory and philosophy into functional practice. The process of melding philosophy and theory generates a general obligation of consistency and a universal prerogative of flexibility. The general obligation is to avoid practices that are incongruent with either the theory or the philosophy chosen. If these two academic operations are related and compatible, there must be a series of instructional operations to serve both and violate neither.

One time while conducting an in-service workshop for a group of elementary teachers one of the authors was faced with a very real dilemma. The group had committed themselves to teaching with an associationistic mode. After choosing a sequential textbook and devising a series of directed graduated experiences with a well-developed reward system, the group raised one last little question. "Now how do we teach them to think creatively on their own using this system?" Some of the teachers were quite reluctant to accept the basic incompatibility of the two sets of mandates. One cannot expect an S-R practice to serve cognitive ends or for cognitive means to be used in the pursuit of associative ends.

Some educators may accept the obligation of consistency with such zealous fervor as to destroy flexibility in the educational process. Psychological theory and educational philosophy can be construed as an awesome pair of masters to be served with fear and trembling. When one serves them instead of using them, a professionally frightening behavior often results — rigidity. A teacher who has worked his way through his theory and his philosophy and has carefully planned and executed a consistent procedure often succumbs to the temptation of constancy. Instead of identifying this procedure as one rational way of teaching, a subtle metamorphosis takes place and it becomes the best and *only* way to teach. All theories and philosophies accept the concept of flexibility. The degree of individualization may vary, but no systems support one method or approach administered exactly the same to all. Variability in approach is expected of the teacher regardless of whether he is using programmed instruction, logical analysis, or transactional participation.

The educator formulating his practice must be aware that

success can have an incipiently disastrous dimension. Too many fine educators have ceased their search for absolute truth, stopped experimenting, or restricted their growth because some initial effort was productive. Your unique and creative extrapolations of the following two sets of principles should always be considered as approximations, not as final statements of the best educational practice that you can generate.

GENERAL ASSOCIATIVE PRINCIPLES

The goal of education is to transmit known natural law to the young. This is best accomplished by a precise shaping of the behavior of youth to be productive members of a technological society.

The conditioning approaches provide an effective model for teaching. By manipulating rewards or reinforcers behavior can become controlled or specified. The most efficient way to teach is to utilize this potentiality for control of behavior to cause learning to occur in the student.

Subject matter is determined by two basic requirements in the scientific society: (1) the knowledge prerequisite for solving current problems, and (2) the data for extending knowledge.

To accomplish the educative goal learners are rewarded or reinforced for studying available knowledge. In addition students are provided with practice in decision making through the use of objective methods of associationism. Decisions based on the external analysis of problems are considered best because real as contrasted with inferential data serves as the basis of problem resolution.

This type of education is self-correcting. Teachers and learners receive information on the effectiveness of their efforts. The curriculum and educational methodology are modified as experimental evidence indicates. As more laws of the universe are discovered, they can be added to the curriculum. Interim educational goals on a local, regional, and national level can be objectively sought and tested for. The process of education becomes one of continual scientific refinement toward the ultimate goal of knowing natural law.

169

RATIONAL EDUCATIONAL PRACTICE

GRADING

Men are motivated by rewards or reinforcers. The associationists have determined that grades operate as motivational factors and afford an increase in performance.

People will work for grades. The grade becomes identified as a tool that can be effectively used to condition behavior. Grades have become a measure of success for realist-oriented pupils and teachers. The achievement and the distribution of grades has become highly motivating for both.

Carefully contrived grades have objective attributes: (1) grade measures derived from normative groups can be quantified and (2) grades have been proven to be reliable predictors of future academic performance. In view of these objective attributes and because performance can be modified through the manipulation of grades, the associationist accepts the grading system as an aid in predicting and controlling classroom behavior.

PACING

The real world has an inherent structure. In order to effectively impart knowledge (the basic task of education) it is necessary that this structure, as it is known today, be presented to the youth of the culture. It is not parsimonious to allow students to explore when they think they must. The educator has at his command a more thorough knowledge of his field and the capabilities of his students. Therefore, it is the teacher who must decide the appropriate rate at which material should be presented.

Psychological research has revealed that the shaping of behavior of learners can be significantly influenced by careful step-by-step sequencing of material and pacing at the organism's optimal rate. Only qualified educators and psychologists can determine the relevance and appropriateness of the programming; the learner does not have the skills necessary to participate in this decision.

Testing

Since the transmission of factual material is the primary business of education, testing the effectiveness of the transmittal is a central problem. The tests used should be quantifiable and should be applicable for a variety of individual learners. A large portion of time is justifiably given to the construction and validation of measures used in examining the amount of knowledge gained by the learner.

Teacher-made tests are useful and desirable. However, such tests are inadequate alone since they do not provide sufficient comparative data. The standardized test supplies such findings. Since standardized instruments are constructed so that they can be used with a wide variety of groups and because these tests tend to focus on factual knowledge, the teacher accomplishes two purposes. (1) He is able to compare his students against a larger, more cosmopolitan sample. (2) He obtains a more objective measure of the factual knowledge that his students can recall.

Testing is done to determine where to begin learning. In addition, testing occurs during the learning process to provide feedback on progress for the student and to give the teacher information that leads to modification of procedures where required. It is crucial to the pacing of instruction that learners are presented material that they can handle. If students are forced to study material that they already know, additional reinforcements will not increase the rate of responding. If, on the other hand, students are presented with material too difficult for them, they will not exhibit right responses that can be rewarded. Without reward their behavior cannot be modified.

Student Participation

The major task of the learner is to be responsive to the expositions of knowledge that the teacher provides. Pure science is the producer of knowledge. The informed educator has an adequate background of knowledge from which to teach. Both the teacher

171

and the learner are consumers of the culture. The teacher directs the learner by conducting field trips, demonstrations, and other types of encounters with factual knowledge. The learner's role in all of this is to honor the reasonable expectations and demands of the teacher. It is the teacher's responsibility to structure the learning experience. The educator must also assume the responsibility for adequately presenting the content of knowledge to the learner. This content is the most significant business of the teacher; all else is secondary. The teacher is the liaison between scientific truth and the learner. Therefore, the teacher encourages the learner to be more and more responsive to the content of learning.

A learner is assumed to be fully participating in the learning experience to the extent that he achieves mastery of the content presented. Differences among learners in terms of response rates are realized and taken into account. As long as the learner is comprehending content consistent with his intelligence, as measured by standardized instruments, he is meeting the expectations of the associationist. Beyond this, any failure on the part of the student to be attentive and responsive mandates an investigation of the effectiveness of the teaching technology employed.

TEACHER-LEARNER PLANNING

The planning of the content presentation is the province of the teacher. Learners are not assumed to be ready to solve problems until they have mastered the necessary subject matter. Beginners in any subject matter area do not have the background and experience to be involved in the selection of material. The sophisticated scholar is not only permitted to plan, he is expected to plan. This person has the knowledge necessary to engage effectively in the planning of the work to be done.

The most important aspect of planning that teachers and learners engage in collectively is an evaluation of the learners' performance. This can provide the learner with a realistic goal. It is important to insure that the student realize where he stands in terms of content mastery. It is also important that he realize what the probabilities are for his success in various scholastic and occupational endeavors. Therefore, learners need to be involved in the planning done by teachers and counselors concerning what aspects of content they should be able to master. Aptitude and intelligence test results together with achievement data should be used to assist the teacher and learner in making the best possible use of the learner's capacity.

It is important to know which students are statistically more liable to be successful in college. It is also important to know for which trades the terminal students are best fitted. Planning has as its base, therefore, the accumulative evidence of years of grading, testing, and reporting on the progress of content mastery. For the associationist the best way to create an effective educational program is to carefully assess the abilities of the students and to assist these people in channeling their capacities into areas where their productivity will be maximized.

DISCIPLINE

Most problems of discipline are reactions to improper placement of students in educational programs and poorly sequenced and paced instruction. The answer to "discipline problems" is to resolve the causative problems. If we expect the human organism to be responsive, we must plan the curriculum so that all learners have the opportunity to exhibit and receive adequate reinforcement for appropriate behavior. There are large numbers of incidental rewards present in the environment that when permitted to become associated with undirected and undesired behavior will interfere with planned learning. If a student is bored by material that is too simple or if he experiences excessive failure, he will respond to incidental reinforcers that will negate the educator's control. For example, a student who is ineffective in the classroom will probably find out of school activities more reinforcing. If this occurs, he might be expected to skip classes, to say he is ill, or to bring inappropriate behavior into the classroom.

Punishment, as a means of controlling inadequate behavior, is ineffective in modifying responses. The only really effective means of securing and maintaining good discipline is to engineer more carefully the learning environment. If content is geared to the capacities of the learners, and if the material is properly sequenced with adequate reinforcement, expected behaviors will be learned and used.

GENERAL FIELD PRINCIPLES

Education is the formal process that facilitates learning. Teaching, which emphasizes almost exclusively the teacher's contribution to the learning process, may better be reserved for associationistic models of instruction. The central theme of facilitation is found in the teacher being an effective person capable of aiding the learner in sharpening his perceptions.

Throughout the general discussion of the field model, one must take care to avoid an easily made misinterpretation. One is not concerned with a licentious experience in which the learner responds to superficial psychological stimulation. Letting him do "his own thing," if that thing is an unexamined commitment, is not the educator's role. Aiding the learner in a personal-social definition of problems with personally relevant resolutions is the primary concern of the instructor.

GRADING

If grading is defined as process in which the performance of a learner is measured quantitatively or ranked subjectively by the instructor, then grading is irrelevant on three counts: First, any assessment made independently by an outside agency is not relevant to the learning process. One does not learn because a good grade is given after learning or because a good grade is anticipated. Second, assuming for the moment that external evaluation is valid for some nonlearning purposes, comparison with groups having little or no relevance for the learner would have no direct bearing or significance for his learning. What difference does it make if 92% of the population solve a problem in 20 minutes? If he solves it in 19 or takes 32 he is no better off knowing what others have done in similar but uniquely different situations. Third, suppose one did not use quantitative measures derived from normative data to grade. What is the advantage for the learner if a teacher subjectively grades a student's efforts at solving personally relevant problems? One of the most dismal grading situations is that of having a creative artistic interpretation (painting or sketch) graded as a "C" work or for that matter in terms of growth as an "A" work.

Grading as a practice may be justified only as an administrative substitution for effective evaluation. In no case can it be said to directly promote the differentiation or reorganization of personal perceptions.

PACING

Proper pacing is vital for effective learning. Pacing is accomplished as the educator and the student fulfill their roles in assuming initiative and responsibility. The student honestly extends himself in the solution of problems that he has accepted as personal. The teacher helps the student reappraise his efforts in terms of his interests and abilities. The learner is not encouraged to take on responsibilities completely at odds with his previous performance, nor is he permitted to see himself as a static organism to be satisfied with previous levels of performance. The proper balance of drive and restraint is maintained in an interactive process between mentor and learner to the extent that they are free to critically communicate with each other.

TESTING

Testing, no matter how formal and quantitative, has little traumatic impact if it is done within a transactional frame of reference. The question investigated is: "Where is the learner in his process of perceptual organization?" It is not: "Where has he failed?" or, "Where has he completed his learning?" Test performance is never the goal of formal instruction. A "testing situation" that tells the individual what he needs to know about his performance leads to a sense of purpose and accomplishment. There are few occasions when finding out whether he is "good" or "good enough" promotes an interactive sense of adequacy.

A more relevant term of assessment is evaluation. The distinction between testing and evaluation is often the difference between passing a test and engaging in a series of critical appraisals. Evaluation suggests not only progress towards goals, but also alternate modes of goal achievement and goal modification.

Rarely can a standardized test or a previously made teacher test fully meet the demands of field evaluation. Much of the complete evaluation must be developed by the instructor and student as a function of the specific situation. Many more forms of communication beyond pencil and paper should be used if the purpose of testing is to inform the learner about his progress and the educator about his effectiveness in facilitating learning.

STUDENT PARTICIPATION

The student is the primary participant in the learning experience. Learning is what *he* does. The problem defined for investigation are those that he believes are relevant. Therefore, the first aspect of the student's role is to examine his personal world for issues that need resolution. A second aspect is to examine the world as perceived by his teacher and others to see if their perceptions of problems have relevance for him. Next, he engages in tentative solutions of the selected problems.

The student, regardless of his age or sophistication, then shares his investigations with his peers and other involved people. Reinterpretations, reassessments, and new approaches evolve as the individual increases his differentiations.

Throughout the whole process of learning, the learner obligates himself to be a thinking individual who assumes the privilege-responsibility of being concerned about himself. He further assumes that the perceptions other people hold may be of some significance. He examines their contributions and bilaterally engages in a process of assimilation and expansion. He is always an involved, responsive, and responsible individual concerned with his personal-social relationships with all the dynamic integrants of his perceived universe.

Teacher-Learner Planning

All learning activities are transactions between teacher and learner. Quite naturally the novice does not perceive or anticipate all of the complexities of a new learning experience. He may not even be aware of its significance. The teacher has an obligation to present alternate perceptions for the learner to evaluate. If they have relevance then any "normal" learner will modify his interpretation with subsequent changes in his field. The teacher responds transactionally by making his personal interpretations available to the students. The student has an obligation to translate and modify any of the teacher's ideas he uses. The more perfect field teacher enthusiastically engages in a reciprocal relationship. He is willing to enlarge and modify his concept of a significant educational experience as the learner is able to communicate needs and problems other than those that the instructor brings to the situation.

The other aspects of planning are also approached with the same style of intervention. Method of attack, resources, performance criteria, and assessment procedures are developed by the same process used in the definition and selection of problems.

Discipline

Discipline, as it is commonly used to denote disturbing, unproductive, antipersonal, antisocial behavior, is a term of negation. It can be dealt with only by altering the original perceptions that give rise to it.

There are three major factors related to undisciplined student and instructor behavior.

1. Classroom conditions perceived as being alien to the best interest of the individual are frequently associated with "bad" behavior.

177

2. Home and community conditions may be threatening with the resultant anxieties and protests carried into the classroom.
3. In some cases pathologies of various types may be related to undisciplined behavior.

Remediation of all three factors is a complex process. The ingenuity and patience of the instructor and the learner may be taxed, but amelioration is usually possible.

Classroom conditions are modifiable in a school that puts the student first. If no out-of-school or pathological factors are operating, the teacher-learner team ought to be able to effect the changes required to make schooling relevant and worthwhile.

Teachers should not extend themselves beyond their experience and education in attempting to correct home or community situations that cause inappropriate school behavior. A more modest approach of engaging all of the social services personnel of the school and the community to assist in these problems is necessary. Compensation in the schoolroom is rarely as effective as correction of the causal factors.

Sociopathic and psychopathic aspects of behavior need to be investigated and therapy prescribed and executed by the professional staff of the school and the community. Extended compassion and the excusing of undisciplined behavior imposes a cruel burden. The person continues to live with his problem; the others in the classroom are victims of the learner's abuse or misuse of class time; the teacher is forced into a therapeutic relationship with only educational skills and background. Students with special problems are entitled to a different type of assistance because their needs are different. Real compassion dictates the correction of pathology before the obligation of transactive participation.

PERSONALIZED PRACTICE

We realize that a presentation of general principles of educational practice leaves the person without specific ways to achieve educational goals in the classroom. Each union of philosophy and theory would demand a unique teaching strategy based on the rational model and the personality of the person teaching. Since a compendium of particularized educational practice does not and probably cannot exist, this volume serves its purpose by involving the reader in the initial phases of establishing personal commitments and styles in teaching.

The expectation is that most readers will continue this process by consulting with their educational colleagues both in professional courses and field situations. Such mutual exploration facilitates the differentiation of educational practice, professional relationships, and responsibilities.

PRIMARY SOURCES FOR FURTHER READING

Combs, Arthur W. ed. *Perceiving, Behaving, Becoming.* Association for Supervision and Curriculum Development: The Association, 1962.

Skinner, B. F. *The Technology of Teaching.* New York: Appleton-Century-Crofts, 1968.

Thorndike, Edward L. *Human Learning.* New York: Century, 1931.

Wertheimer, Max. *Productive Thinking.* New York: Harper, 1959.

SECONDARY SOURCES AND COLLECTIONS OF READINGS

Fargo, G. A., Behrns, C., and Nolan, P. eds. *Behavior Modification in the Classroom.* New York: Wadsworth, 1970.

Hamachek, D. ed. *Human Dynamics in Psychology and Education.* Boston: Allyn and Bacon, 1968.

Procrustean Predilections or Popular Hang-ups in Education

Contemporary American educational practice is a composite of classical and modern forces sometimes amalgamated in highly unlikely permutations. In this section we offer you a number of contemporary ideas in education that have developed from the bowdlerization of cogent formal philosophies and theories. The purpose of this section is to provide each reader an opportunity to apply his critical skills in detecting the basic philosophical bent inherent in a description of educational practices and to divine the implicit or explicit assumptions made about learning. Perhaps all the more insidious because these beliefs and practices can be stated as reasonable common-sense interpretations, each of the following sets of assumptions in our opinion fails to meet the criterion of being consistent with compatible theory and philosophy.

Although we ask a few questions about each practice, we hope that you will have many meaningful questions to raise as well.

When you feel ready to tackle a sample of current problems in teaching practice, please turn the page.

TREAT THEM NICELY

One of the most pleasant distortions of an educational philosophy is found in some nursery and elementary schools in which the stated or implied function of education is to treat the children nicely so that they may grow up free of restriction or inhibition. This "rosebud" school of thought sees each child as a perfect miniaturization of an adult, who only needs the opportunity to unfold into the full flower of adulthood. For the very cynical it appears that much of the teacher's contrived "niceness" seems to fit into this colorful analogy as the "manure" used to foster growth and development. The defense or denial of such a position about the purposes of teaching should rest more on what this approach means in the overall interpretation about the nature of man, society, and education rather than on the individual teacher's desire to be known as a nice person, or his wish to treat the children with total sweetness, or the children's wish to receive such treatment.

Questions

1. Do these assumptions about the growing nature of the child fit any of the three philosophies discussed in Set Two "Formulations"?

2. Does the permissiveness of this position coordinate with biological or motivational assumptions of any of the four theoretical systems of Set Three "Sciences and Systems"?

3. If this attitude toward education is wholly or partly compatible with a philosophy and a theory, are the theory and philosophy compatible according to the analysis presented in Set Four "Congruent Philosophies and Theories"?

MAKE THEM DO IT

From the very distant past comes a point of view that has often become separated from the rationale that made it fit other cultures at other times. The present statement would be: "It is important for children to learn to do certain things irrespective of their interests and regardless of whether they see any reason to learn them because these are the things that everyone ought to know." Tallying the number of translations from the Latin, the number of identical sunsets painted by second grade children, or for that matter the number of educational surveys and canned experiments passively conducted by college students, would tax the capacity of the largest computers we have. However, we may relax because the teachers involved know these are the best things to do and all will be better for having done them.

Questions

1. It is obvious that this practice is based on certain classical ideas about the nature of education. Could one support the proposition that this is also compatible with traditional assumptions about the nature of man and society?

2. Is it really consistent with the intent and purpose of the classical Greek concepts of education?

3. Does the notion of "making" people learn meet the essential conditions of learning as defined by either the field or associationist theoreticians?

MAKE THEM DO THE RIGHT THING

In effect this is the same type of approach as "Make Them Do It," except that it adds the teacher's private interpretation of what is Godly and righteous.

Some groups emphasizing drug usage are adopting the accoutrements and identifications of formal religious institutions. A brand new question posed for our society is, Should sincere, confirmed drug-user-teachers be permitted to advocate a child's use of drugs as part of a religious experience? An old question still unresolved is, Should teachers with more conventional religious identifications be permitted to teach that all expression of heterosexuality before marriage should be avoided because of the teacher's personal concepts of immorality? A differentiation must be made between the educational philosopher who adopts a coherent theistic ethic and the teacher who imposes private moralistic connotations and denotations that go beyond classical and contemporary religious systems. The privately moralistic teacher determines on a personal basis that it is the duty of children to learn certain modes of behavior, that it is wicked to have independent thought, naughty to disagree with the teacher, or proper to be passive and accepting of the teacher's authority. Such teachers are most easily detected when their values and teachings are at odds with community mores and values. Usually they do not concern themselves with what others think of their missionary work and seldom modify their actions in terms of new information about children or the society in which they live.

Questions

1. What would it take to move this teaching behavior out of the domain of the private interpretation into the realm of a classical foundation of eternal truth?

2. Could Thorndike or Skinner, who both believe in the strict management of learning outcomes, support such a formulation?

MAKE THEM DO THE HARD THING

The learner ought to do that which is difficult because hard work is better for him. To avoid the risk of doing easy things, most teachers who rely on this "philosophical" position also eliminate pleasant activities and hold in great suspicion that which students grasp easily. A most common practice that must have "hardness" as a prime component is that of giving students lower marks at the beginning of the semester so that they will work harder. No matter how effective his performance the learner must adopt the notion that learning is not easy under any circumstances, that he is in jeopardy of failure unless he tries harder. Many teachers defend this practice by stating that they can later give more high marks and thereby increase motivation as material becomes more difficult. Students, however, develop some extremely intelligent defensive techniques to circumvent the impact of this approach. For years a required experience in many teacher education sequences has been performance on the piano. Music students with recital experience quickly learn to come into the pretest and exhibit great difficulty in attempting to play "Mary Had a Little Lamb." Since this sets a low first performance standard, by mid-semester they are able to show tremendous growth by playing simple pieces for a "C" and move to complex songs by the end of the semester for an "A". Imagine the plight of the teacher who really has to learn to play in this same semester!

Questions

1. Define the students' responses to this situation in phenomenological terms.

2. Does the withholding of high grades meet the social ethics of the technological formulation in which the social ends justify the means to reach those ends?

MAKE SCHOOL A PLEASANT EXPERIENCE

Fortunately, education has an antidote to the teacher whose purpose it is to make students learn—the teacher who is committed to joyous expression. All school experiences must be the free expression of personal emotional satisfaction. The motto emblazoned on the social programs that serve as curriculum guides for teachers of this order must be, "Let them have fun." If it is not fun then it is too real and earnest to be a part of the experience of the young. Ultimate success resides in the child's opportunity to experience the real or imaginary benefits of being happy all the time.

One of the most well-intentioned groups that are most subject to this error are those kindergarten teachers who see their primary role as mother substitute. They perceive that the primary function of preschool education is to provide a series of pleasant recreational activities. The function appears to be one of a state of intellectual suspended animation between home experiences and formal schooling in the first grade. The teachers in this category must be distinguished from the group of early childhood educators who use the child's present interests, problems, and developmental tasks as the basis of the curriculum. The latter group uses play as a focal point in a series of learning experiences. The "fun" teachers emphasize the emotional responses to activities that do not accentuate the academic responsibility of the learner.

Questions

1. How does uncritical play fail to prepare a child to participate now in a transactional society?

2. Which of the four theories would find this free play concept unacceptable or undesirable? Why?

LET THEM EXPERIENCE LIFE AS AN EXPERIMENT

Providing a relief if not a balance for the "happy" school of thought is the modern teacher who has taken up the mantle of the earlier day religionists and tries to save the world and society and children by insisting that children be taught to do things the right way. The right way in this case is the SCIENTIFIC way. The assumption seems to be either that all truth can be discovered with science and in science or that anything not amenable to analysis with the present methods of science is unknowable and therefore insignificant. Often the most capricious behavior is disguised as an experiment. Two hallmarks separate this false prophet of science from the gentlemen and scholars of science. The first is the rally call, "Let's see what happens." This call must be given just a moment before some action and must never give rise to a period of inquiry about the implications of the prior experiences of others or the impact of the indicated action. The second indicator is the extent to which the "experiments" are left unreported, unwritten, unanalyzed, and unshared. Instead of contributing to a growing body of knowledge the experience seems to satisfy only irrational curiosity. Perhaps the comment, "Wasn't that interesting?" is a suitable substitute for scholarship, but it would not satisfy those who believe more systematically in philosophies of science or scientific educational philosophies.

Questions

1. How does such an approach provide for organizing and integrating perceptions in a Gestalt frame of reference?

2. What congruence is there between the "content" of this type of experience and the content criteria of each of the three philosophies discussed?

TELL THEM AND TEST THEM

This is probably the most widely practiced teaching technique based on the unexamined assumption that one learns by listening. It is broadly applied in school, home, church, and elsewhere as a formal and informal method of instruction. If this is a "bad" method then most of us have been subjected to an endless stream of bad teaching. Inherent in such as approach, however, is the notion that when we tell a person something he ought to remember it because it is good for him, or because he is a recipient of everything that is presented to him, or because we believe it is important and presume the learner will so perceive.

Questions:

1. Are these justifications consistent with any educational philosophy?

194

2. Are these statements more compatible with field or associationist theories?

3. Are these three justifications "differing" or "disagreeing" statements according to principles used in Set Three "Sciences and Systems"?

TEST THEM ON RESEARCH

A popular idea in our modern superscientific culture. Basic to such an approach may be either or both of the following ideas:

1. "Science is the one viable way to find out about reality. Experimental research is the only truth we can count on. Scientific investigation is the epitome of human experience. Our society got where it is by being scientific; therefore let us work in education to perpetuate this social order."

2. "Since I have finished my training as a researcher, I think research is great and I know my students should learn to enjoy it too. Nothing is worthwhile if it is not complex, and research is a complex exercise."

As pure in intent and noble of purpose as these statements may be, they happen to coincide with neither ethical systems nor experimental evidence. Such statements undoubtedly are inspirational for some and good clean fun for others, but do fail the criteria of being consistent with the common-core values of society or the information available about how or why people learn.

Questions:

1. What would the transactive rebuttal be for these two concepts?

2. What are the teacher-learner planning implications of these two views for the associationist and field models of learning?

HAVE THEM LOOK, SEE, AND SAY

This is a form of simplistic approach which has been espoused as being a "natural" approach to education. In this type of classroom the emphasis seems to be on getting everybody to talk about their personal experiences or common activities. Talking is expected to cause or promote worthwhile learning. Structure is virtually absent. Some typical justifications are: This is the way we learned before education became such a formalized process. This is a free and spontaneous way to learn. It is the natural way children learn before they come to school. The learner is given an opportunity to express himself.

There are problems with this technique. What does the teacher do when the spontaneity breaks down? Is any endeavor allowable? If not, what are the limits of acceptable behavior? How would personal and social limits be structured in a supposedly free and natural classroom?

Questions:

1. Which philosophy is most disposed toward naturalism and how would the "look, see, and say" method be regarded as an educational tool?

2. To what extent would such an approach facilitate or inhibit pacing?

PRAISE THEM AND PUNISH THEM

A time-honored technique of teaching. If it were not for the fact that we have direct evidence that punishment techniques result in very little positive change in behavior, this technique would be compatible with some of the educational philosophies and theories of learning. There is, however, a much more common distortion of this approach, which is malignant beyond compare because of its subtlety. The teacher uses praise and punishment to indicate his personal pleasure with the learner's performance. This use is tantamount to emotional blackmail and is contrary to the spirit or outcomes of research on human learning.

Until teachers will take the time to represcribe the daily goals of education and develop techniques of measuring how well children are meeting these goals one can expect teachers to continue in the pattern of saying, "I like it," or "I don't" instead of properly evaluating student performance.

Questions:

1. What has to be done to make praise and punishment an adequate basis for instructional technology?

2. With which of your points would a Skinnerian take exception?

PROCRUSTEAN PREDILECTIONS

SUBTLY PERSUADE THEM

Get students to do what you have already decided they should learn. If you can make students believe that the activity is their idea you will have them in the palm of your hand.

This approach appeals to certain pseudopsychologically oriented instructors, because it appears to take in account the motivational state of the learner. The extent to which this information can be misunderstood is indicated in the following anecdote. One of the authors was invited to witness a very up-to-date approach to classroom instruction by a sincere student teacher. The main purpose of the lesson was to illustrate how well he could put into practice some of the field theory concepts being discussed in class. He already had a developed lesson plan involving the history of England. Convinced he should no longer make the students learn things they did not want to learn he started his lesson in the following way:

"Good morning boys and girls."

"Good morning Mr. Jones."

"I bet you kids really like animals don't you?"

"Yes!"

"What kinds of animals do you like?"

"Dogs." "Cats." "Horses." "Cows."

"What about zoo animals?"

"Lions!" "Tigers!" "Bears!"

"Hey, that's great! Did you know there is a lion on the great seal of England? I know you are going to enjoy this lesson on the English Parliament!"

The questions: Did he do right? Did he do wrong? Did he do the right thing wrong? The answers to these and other important questions depend entirely on your interpretation of the art and science of education.

If we have failed to cite your favorite target for criticism feel free to use this page to note your own examples of people who do things without overt regard for rational reasons. Better yet, perhaps it would be interesting for you to declare your own educational strategy and review it in terms of what you have read or will read.

Evolving Issues

THE EVOLUTIONARY PROCESS

Any book once it is written is immediately out of date if it purports to deal with current affairs. Education is a very current affair and any discussion or description has only transitory validity. The most timely information about educational change is probably in today's newspaper or on television or radio at this moment. A more profound discussion of the educational change process of six months or a year ago is probably tucked away in some partially read professional magazine or journal. Tomorrow's change is an idea someone has today.

The process of educational change is engendered and perpetuated by three causal dynamics.

1. There are a number of old questions in education that have never been answered adequately. Yet teachers and teaching institutions must go on with their educational programs just as if they knew what they were doing in these areas. New teachers and conscientious, experienced teachers maintain an incessant hue and cry for information. As understanding of the learning process and the impact of education expands, new techniques

must be developed to support the answers being found for the previously unanswered questions.

2. The extension of knowledge about and concern for education has resulted in philosophical and experimental reexaminations of old answers to old questions in education. Many of these formulations at one time were both significant and relevant. Changing social conditions and new knowledge have resulted in some old answers being discarded. Of even more dramatic impact is the fact that some old problems or questions are now of only the most academic interest. Changing conditions have dissipated the impact of some previously critical educational questions as surely as they have diminished the demand for kerosene stereoptican machines.

3. The corollary of old answers and questions being outdated is the emergence of questions that have never existed before. Technological changes in particular have generated both the need for new and better statements of problems and the need for contemporary answers. The questions of the effective use of television was insignificant before mass production of television sets and the establishment of educational purposes and programs. The question has in fact already been modified to include study of differential effects of color and black and white programming.

OPEN ISSUES: EXTANT AND EMERGENT

EXTANTS

Some old questions relating to man's innate postures and capacities remain unanswered. Two perennial issues are the biology of learning and the nature of "humanness."

The science of man has no way of independently determining man's basic nature. Various ideas of human posture have been proposed. All of these must remain open issues today, since their fundamental premises cannot be adequately tested for accuracy.

Man is variously described as active, reactive, and interactive. Twentieth century science predisposes an interpretation of man as a neutral organism rather than either negative or positive. The "rightness" of such notions depends solely on the philosophical system chosen. A number of contradictory assumptions have been made, but science has not empirically validated or invalidated them.

Thousands of experiments have been conducted on infrahuman organisms by biologists, psychologists, physiologists, and others. Some of these studies have even utilized such simple organisms as the lowly planarian. Although our knowledge of human electrochemical processes has advanced enormously, we are not far enough beyond Plato's men-of-iron and men-of-gold level of description to make definitive statements about biological processes of learning. In fact, learning theorists seldom make their statements in biochemically relevant terms. Perhaps this is their way of saying that they have no definitive way of knowing with our present science the practical implications of the known biological corollaries of learning.

Extant and Reemerging Problems

As we face old questions still unanswered, we likewise face old answers seldom questioned. In a variety of ways some of these once quiescent issues are being raised today. Is learning primarily of one type as most theories suggest? Is one level of description of learning adequate for all our purposes? Do we all need a compulsory formal education for ten or twelve years? Is the age of four or five really the most effective time to begin formal education?

Field theorists and associationists are equally confident or equally guilty of suggesting that education need concern itself with one level of learning. The responsibilities for educating the above and below average, the disadvantaged and the handicapped have called for a reexamination of this basic premise. It may well be that a number of levels and kinds of learning, including the biochemical, are required to define the scope of formal education. We are too close to this problem to anticipate the outcome.

207

EVOLVING ISSUES

What is the "right" kind and amount of education? When should formal education begin? These two questions are being discussed again. Many educators and critics today are questioning what part of the educative experience is or should be perceived as personally relevant to the individual learner. Do noncollege-bound students need an education that is essentially college preparatory in nature? Since the time of Thorndike's monumental work on transfer of learning, the theoretical answer has been "no"; yet looking at the school curriculum it might as well have been "yes." Curricula are still highly oriented toward a classical education model, which may not be relevant for even the college preparatory student. Students have had little involvement with curriculum or the determination of personalized courses of study. The educational value of stereotyped educational experience is being sharply questioned on the campus, in the ghettos, and perhaps soon in suburbia.

The problem of the best time to begin public education has been revivified as the nation reviews the successes and failures of federal programs of preschool education. Some of these young learners have profited in some ways from the experiences given them. The logical question then becomes: Should all children have the advantages of starting their formal education earlier?

EMERGENTS

The growing impact of existential philosophy on psychology and education may be precipitating some of the most troublesome yet exciting and challenging problems of our time. Many students on the college scene today are gripped by existential thought. Some react to the idea of one's ultimate valuing of his own behavior by interpreting it as a licentious "do as I please" notion. Others see the question of valuing existentially as "doing as I feel I need to do *with* responsibility." This latter approach says that man is becoming. He is becoming aware of his autonomy and the concomitant responsibility. As man makes this autonomous choice he must consider who he is. As a person views himself from all perspectives he is transcending the limits of his present state. He is continually reexamining his "becomingness." Through this transcendence, man becomes involved in the human predicament. Man must care. It would be difficult to deny that the contemporary college student cares more overtly than his predecessors. He is a continual source of embarrassment to those who seek to maintain things as they were—tranquil, blended together in dedicated quietude.

What revisions of curriculum and methodology would accomplish existential purposes? What does this philosophical attitude mean for our twentieth century scientific culture? Would an existential approach to the science of man and the education of youth raise us to new heights of human growth, or would it destroy what we have and provide us with an anarchical social situation?

Even as our philosophy expands, so does our technology. In this electronic age the computer has developed quasi-human characteristics. What does this mean for our educational enterprise? Computers are being developed that can interact or at least make complex reactions. Can these machines "teach" as well as present material? Will they ever become "educators"? With the further evolution of these machines many new questions will be raised. CAI or computer assisted instruction is already a reality on many college campuses and in some experimental public schools. Will CAI be able to promote initiative and creativity as effectively as the human teacher? Are there cognitive dimensions of thinking the computer can "teach" as well as it presents factual material? Can a machine be programmed to support creative responses that it has not yet performed or stored? If some of these questions are partially or wholly answered in the affirmative, will this mean that teachers must be able to use computer language and logic as they now use a teacher's manual or slide projector? Should a great deal of teaching be done by means of computer to free the teacher to interact with students on an individual and small-group basis?

What does the electronic age mean for school attendance? Need children congregate at great public expense in a special building or can the "school of the mother's knee" be expanded by augmenting mother with a television knob or computer terminal? If some or all of the above are affirmed what will be done if it is discovered that half the population completes formal instruction, now thought of as required for high school graduation, in signifi-

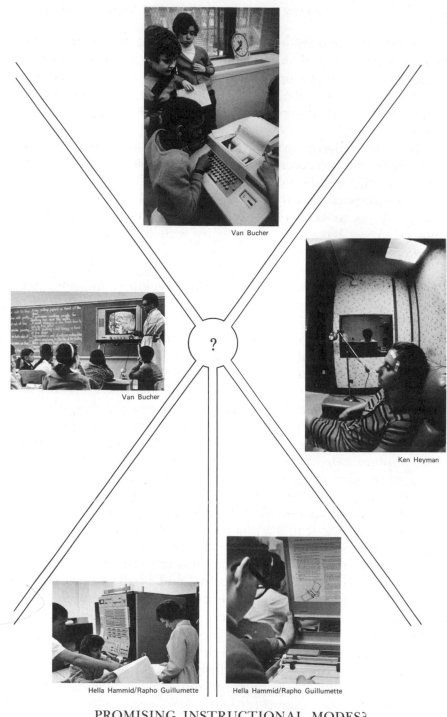

Van Bucher

Van Bucher

Ken Heyman

Hella Hammid/Rapho Guillumette

Hella Hammid/Rapho Guillumette

PROMISING INSTRUCTIONAL MODES?

cantly less time (because education becomes individualized and because the learner has access to the "continuous" attention of a computer)?

The computer is not the only technological explosion that has come upon us. Consider the issue of drugs and "mind expansion." Scientific research on the effects of LSD and other mind-expansion drugs has been carried on for years. In the latter half of the 1960s the use of hallucinogens and other preparations moved out of the laboratory and into the hands of college students, teenagers, and others. What will this investigation bring with it? Some say a nightmare for our whole society. Others say a new order. Is it possible that an increase in controlled study of chemical states of the human organism will disclose positive and permanent methods of improving brain function? Can the receptiveness of the human brain be increased by chemical means to better utilize the speed and complexity of computer programming of information and thought processes?

The earlier delineation in this book of dealing with current practice denies us the privilege of limitless wishful thinking or guessing about the future of educational practice. The disadvantage of writing in the present precludes an unlimited view of the future of education. The reader with the advantage of looking ahead at a later date will probably see more clearly than we have seen the issues that we have chosen to include. Fortunately for the profession he will probably perceive and resolve issues that we have not even anticipated.

SELECTIONS FOR FURTHER EXPLORATION

Gerard, Ralph W. in Atkinson, Richard C. and Wilson, H. A. eds. *Computer Assisted Instruction*. New York: Academic Press, 1969, pp. 15–39.

Glass, Bentley. "Evolution in Human Hands." *Phi Delta Kappan,* May 1969, pp. 506–510.

Jourard, Sidney M. *Disclosing Man to Himself*. Chapter 5. "Growing Experience and the Experience of Growth." Princeton: Van Nostrand, 1968, pp. 152–172.

Krech, David. "Psychoneurobiochemeducation." *Phi Delta Kappan,* March 1969, pp. 370–375.

Leonard, George B. *Education and Ecstasy.* New York: Delacorte, 1968.

McConnell, James V. "Memory Transfer through Cannibalism in Planaria." *Journal of Neuropsychiatry,* 1963, **3,** p. 45.

Montague, Ashley. *The Direction of Human Development; Biological and Social Bases.* New York: Harper and Row, 1955.

Morris, Van Cleve. *Existentialism in Education: What It Means.* New York: Harper and Row, 1966.

Olds, James. "Self Stimulation of the Brain." *Science,* 1958, **127,** pp. 315–324.

Rogers, Carl R. *Freedom to Learn.* Columbus, Ohio: Charles E. Merrill, 1969.

Skinner, B. F. *Walden Two.* New York: Macmillan, 1948.

Suppes, Patrick. "Computer Technology and the Future of Education." *Phi Delta Kappan,* April 1968, pp. 420–423.

Summaries
and
Syntheses

PHILOSOPHICAL ISSUES MATRIX

Concepts	Traditional	Technological	Transactional
Man			
potential	Ability to know truth (23) [1:81]	Comprehension of natural law (34) [8:19]	Capacity for social interaction (47) [12:14]
morality	Consistency with truth (25) [4:135]	Harmony with scientific truth (35) [5:14]	Synonymous with social maturity (49) [11:138]
response made	Contemplation of reality (26) [4:27]	Complex mechanical reasoning (35) [7:28]	Social interaction (50) [9:102]
Society			
structure	Stabilized institutions (27) [3:317]	Evolving toward a natural state (36) [8:58]	Dynamic process (51) [11:180]
authority	Assigned roles (27) [3:321]	Competency in science (37) [8:21]	Social endorsement (52) [11:164]
mobility	Controlled and restricted (28) [3:319]	Reward for approved behavior (38) [8:64]	Horizontal movement toward complex relationships (53) [12:24]
communication	Prescribed (29) [4:303]	Structured process (39) [6:31]	Shared social experience (54) [12:4]

PHILOSOPHICAL ISSUES MATRIX (Cont.)

Concepts	Traditional	Technological	Transactional
responsibility	Predetermined code (29) [2:310]	Function of social role (39) [8:67]	Participatory involvement and growth (55) [9:174]
ethics	Ends justify means (30) [2:308]	Relevant means justified by social ends (40) [5:Ch. 6]	Relevant means for tentative ends (56) [12:119]
Education objectives	Knowledge of truth (31) [2:300]	Discovery and application of natural law (41) [7:156]	Personal and societal growth (58) [12:115]
goal determination	Accord with truth (31) [2:330]	Obedience to natural law (42) [7:159]	Transactional relevance (60) [12:126]
content criteria	Reflection of absolutes (32) [1:Ch. 5]	Congruence with objective reality (43) [7:178]	Opportunity for personal-social growth (63) [12:Ch. 9]
social function	Perpetuate stable society (32) [4:141]	Experimental refinement of society (45) [8:81]	Enrichment of self and society (65) [10:125]
learner's role	Active acceptance (33) [4:43]	Reception of knowledge (45) [8:133]	Responsible participation (66) [10:123]

( ) page reference this volume
[ ] primary source reference (see next page)

PRIMARY SOURCES FOR PHILOSOPHICAL ISSUES MATRIX

Traditional Formulations

1. Hutchins, Robert M. *The Conflict in Education.* New York: Harper, 1953.
2. Kant, Immanuel. *The Fundamental Principles of the Metaphysics of Morals* in Vol. 32. *The Harvard Classics.* New York: Collier, 1938.
3. Plato. *The Republic.* Vol. 1. Cambridge: Harvard University Press, 1930.
4. Plato. *The Republic.* Vol. 2. Cambridge: Harvard University Press, 1930.

Technological Formulations

5. Bestor, Arthur. *Educational Wastelands.* Urbana, Illinois: University of Illinois Press, 1953.

6. Bridgman, P. W. *The Logic of Modern Physics*. New York: Macmillan, 1927.
7. Council for Basic Education. *The Case for Basic Education*. Boston: Atlantic–Little, Brown, 1959.
8. Rickover, Hyman. *Education and Freedom*. New York: Dutton, 1959.

TRANSACTIONAL FORMULATIONS

9. Brameld, Theodore. *Toward a Reconstructed Philosophy of Education*. New York: Dryden Press, 1956.
10. Bruner, Jerome. *On Knowing: Essays for the Left Hand*. New York: Athenium, 1965.
11. Childs, John L. *Education and Morals*. New York: Appleton-Century-Crofts, 1950.
12. Dewey, John. *Democracy and Education*. New York: Macmillan, 1916.

LEARNING THEORY SUMMARIES

	Motivational Contingencies	Learning Paradigm	Facilitation Strategy
Thorndike	Frequency, recency, and relevancy of rewards (80) [9:125]	A reward acts to strengthen the connection between a stimulus and a response (81) [9:122]	Management of rewards in a structured situation (82) [7:146]
Skinner	Sequencing and timing of reinforcements (87) [6:145]	A reinforcements increases the probability of a response reoccuring (88) [5:65]	Programmed learning (91) [6:64]
Gestalt	Degrees of perceived ambiguity (99) [3:554]	Reorganization of perceptions (100) [3:550]	Structured ambiguity (102) [2:261]
Combs and Snygg	Sense of personal adequacy (108) [1:56]	Differentiation of the phenomenal field (109) [1:190]	Transactional challenge (111) [1:384]

LEARNING THEORY SUMMARIES (Cont.)

	Biological Capacities	Transfer Functions	Retention Variables
Thorndike	Number of potential S-R bonds (84) [8:309]	Identical and similar elements (85) [8:351,426]	Law of use and disuse (85) [7:2]
Skinner	Undiscriminated biological factors related to response rates (94) [5:31]	Identical and similar operants (94) [5:94]	Schedules of reinforcement (95) [5:70]
Gestalt	Physiological corollaries of perception (103) [4:301]	Transposition of principles and concepts (104) [2:151]	Functional validity (106) [4:178]
Combs and Snygg	Physical potential for growth and differentiation (112) [1:210]	Generalization of perceptual relationships (115) [1:196]	Personal-social relevance (117) [1:200]

( ) page reference this volume
[ ] primary source reference (see p. 220)

PRIMARY REFERENCES FOR LEARNING THEORY SUMMARIES

1. Combs, Arthur W., and Snygg, Donald. *Individual Behavior.* rev. ed. New York: Harper, 1959.
2. Koffka, Kurt. *Growth of the Mind.* London: Kegan, Paul, Trench, Trubner, and Co., Ltd., 1924.
3. Koffka, Kurt. *Principles of Gestalt Psychology.* New York: Harcourt-Brace, 1935.
4. Kohler, Wolfgang. *Gestalt Psychology.* New York: Mentor, 1947.
5. Skinner, B. F. *Science and Human Behavior.* New York: Macmillan, 1953.
6. Skinner, B. F. *Technology of Teaching.* New York: Appleton-Century-Crofts, 1968.
7. Thorndike, Edward L. *Educational Psychology.* Vol. II. New York: Teachers College Columbia, 1914.
8. Thorndike, Edward L. *Educational Psychology.* Vol. III. New York: Teachers College Columbia, 1914.
9. Thorndike, Edward L. *Human Learning.* New York: Century, 1931.

EDUCATIONAL PHILOSOPHIES AND LEARNING SYSTEMS

TABLE OF CONGRUENCE BETWEEN
EDUCATIONAL PHILOSOPHIES AND LEARNING SYSTEMS

Learning Systems	Philosophies		
	Traditional	Technological	Transactional
Thorndike			
Motivation	C (126)	C (126)	I (127)
Learning	C (133)	C (133)	I (133)
Facilitation	C (139)	C (140)	I (140)
Capacity	I (147)	C (147)	I (148)
Transfer	C (153)	C (153)	I (154)
Retention	PA (160)	C (161)	I (161)
Skinner			
Motivation	C (127)	C (127)	I (128)
Learning	C (134)	C (134)	I (134)
Facilitation	C (141)	C (141)	I (142)
Capacity	I (148)	C (148)	PA (149)
Transfer	C (154)	C (154)	I (154)
Retention	PA (162)	C (162)	I (162)
Gestalt			
Motivation	PA (128)	I (129)	C (130)
Learning	I (135)	PA (135)	C (135)
Facilitation	I (143)	I (143)	C (144)
Capacity	PA (149)	I (150)	C (150)
Transfer	PA (156)	I (156)	C (157)
Retention	I (163)	I (163)	C (164)
Combs and Snygg			
Motivation	I (130)	I (131)	C (131)
Learning	I (137)	I (137)	C (137)
Facilitation	I (145)	I (145)	C (145)
Capacity	I (151)	I (151)	C (151)
Transfer	PA (158)	I (159)	C (159)
Retention	I (165)	I (165)	C (165)

C   congruent
I   incongruent
PA   partial agreement
(   ) page reference this volume

SUMMARIES AND SYNTHESES

GENERAL PRINCIPLES OF EDUCATIONAL PRACTICE

Associative Model		Field Model
	Grading	
Effective motivator if objectively derived and impartially distributed (170)		Administrative procedure unrelated to perceptual learning (174)
	Pacing	
Inherent structure of knowledge presented at appropriate rate for the learner (170)		Interactive thrust of concerned educator and involved learner (175)
	Testing	
Measurement or indication of success of transmission of information (171)		Inter-personal assessment by instructor and student of goal validity and approximation (175)
	Student Participation	
Responsive acceptance of professional direction (171)		Assumption of initiative and responsibility for personal involvement (176)
	Teacher-Learner Planning	
Search for inherent structure of content and method (172)		A coordinate transaction (177)
	Discipline	
A behavioral response to proper management of variables in the educational program (173)		Function of personal identification and involvement in self relevant processes (177)

( ) page reference this volume